ENDORSEMENTS

Imagine being an eyewitness to history in advance. Few have ever studied the Day of the Lord, but my spiritual son David Jones was there! It dramatically changed his life forever and will do the same for you.

SID ROTH
Host, *It's Supernatural!*

I have ministered with David Jones and can tell you that David's revelation is the real deal. Prepare to have your world rocked as you read jaw-dropping accounts of what is coming and how to prepare for it.

DAVID HERZOG
President of DHM
www.thegloryzone.org
Author of *Glory Invasion*

David Jones has received the word of the Lord! Second Chronicles 20:20 encourages us to *"Believe in the Lord your God, and you shall be established; believe His prophets, and you shall prosper"* (NKJV). This passage refers to 20/20 vision. In the day and hour in which we live, we need to hear the Lord clearly and believe His Word. But we also need to believe the Lord's prophets, for this will enable us to prosper in any circumstance. This powerful book, *They Thought They Had More Time*, is a prophetic word for the whole world. Believe in the Lord. Believe in this prophetic word, and you will be positioned to prosper in the greatest way imaginable. This timely book can help you develop 20/20 spiritual vision.

KEVIN BASCONI
King of Glory Ministries International

THEY
THOUGHT
THEY HAD
MORE TIME

THEY
THOUGHT
THEY HAD
MORE TIME

I saw the day of the Lord

David Jones

DESTINY IMAGE₀ PUBLISHERS, INC.
P.O. Box 310, Shippensburg, PA 17257-0310
"Promoting Inspired Lives"

This book and all other Destiny Image, Revival Press, MercyPlace, Fresh Bread, Destiny Image Fiction, and Treasure House books are available at Christian bookstores and distributors worldwide.

For more information on foreign distributors, call 717-532-3040.
Reach us on the Internet: www.destinyimage.com.

ISBN TP: 978-0-7684-0321-3
ISBN Ebook: 978-0-7684-8608-7

For Worldwide Distribution, Printed in the U.S.A.
2 3 4 5 6 7 / 17 16 15 14

DEDICATION

This book is dedicated, with a great sense of gratitude and appreciation, to my spiritual dad, Sid Roth, who encouraged me to write this book and to share with the world the vision and message that God gave me of the soon to come "Day of the Lord."

ACKNOWLEDGMENT

A very special thank you to my wife, Suzie Jones, who has always loved me, encouraged me, and stood by my side. Without her help, support, and tireless dedication, the writing and publishing of this book would not have been possible. I could not have asked for a better partner in life.

IMPARTATION

It is my sincere desire that the words contained in this book impart unto you the overwhelming sense of urgency I feel in my spirit over the need for all of us to be ready for the imminent return of the Lord Jesus Christ.

CONTENTS

FOREWORD

GOD HAS ALWAYS USED OPEN VISIONS FOR SPECIAL ASSIGN-ments. In Acts 9, Saul (who became the apostle Paul) journeyed from Jerusalem to Damascus and saw a light from Heaven that was brighter than the sun in the middle of the day, and it brought him to his knees. The voice of our Lord Jesus Christ spoke to him concerning his destiny and the things that he would suffer for the ministry's sake.

In Acts 22:17-18, Paul was praying in a Jerusalem temple, where he says he was in a trance. Jesus told him to get out of Jerusalem because his testimony would not be received. Then, in Acts 23:11, Jesus came in the night and stood by Paul and said to him, *"Be of good cheer, Paul: for as thou hast testified of me in Jerusalem, so must thou bear witness also at Rome."*

There are chosen men and women in the Body of Christ upon whom God releases sovereign grace. He takes them in open visions to show them the things that will come to pass. The Word of God speaks of the word of His wisdom, the unborn future. God has chosen David Jones for such a role in this hour.

I accepted Christ in 1967, and since then I have heard many great men teach on the end of time after studying the prophetic Scriptures. It is one thing to read and compare Scripture to Scripture, but it is a whole deeper dimension of grace and faith to actually see the events of the future before their time. Reading about the end times in Scripture is wonderful, but to personally experience the things that will shortly come to pass because the Holy Spirit takes you there and then to come back to the present time to declare what you have seen is something else entirely.

This summer I sat for three weeks hearing David Jones declare to our church the open vision that he experienced of the end of time. Each night it brought me to a place of searching my own heart to make sure that my ways please God Almighty. A spirit of revival came that caused much weeping and travail at the altar, as well as a harvest of souls coming into the kingdom of God. And that spirit of revival is still in the midst of our local congregation.

As this man preached that time was running out and told of the chaos and the fearful and cataclysmic times he saw the people on the earth experiencing, a spirit of repentance fell upon the congregation. I could personally see in my heart and mind a world being judged by God because it was not prepared for His coming.

I have never heard a man preach the end of time and the coming of Jesus with so much passion and fear of the judgment as David Jones declared. This book will supernaturally prepare you for the coming of the Lord.

The very last thing I remember from the three-week revival was hearing David say each night that people with terror and horror on their faces cried out, "I thought I still had time!" And then it was over! David Jones has been sent to declare to the Body of Christ that the end may happen even before you finish reading this book. We are truly in that season!

BISHOP DWIGHT PATE
Church Point Ministries
Baton Rouge, Louisiana

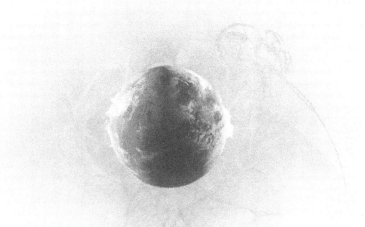

Son of man, the people of Israel are saying, "He's talking about the distant future. His visions won't come true for a long, long time." Therefore, tell them, "This is what the Sovereign Lord says: No more delay! I will now do everything I have threatened. I, the Sovereign Lord, have spoken!" (Ezekiel 12:27-28 NLT)

I SAW THE DAY
OF THE LORD

ONE MORNING A FEW MONTHS AGO, IT FELT LIKE SOMEONE came, took me by the arm, and shook me awake. Instantly, I found myself catapulted into the future in an open vision of the Day of the Lord. At first, as I was hovering over the earth, all seemed well. I could see the beautiful, clear, blue skies, the different ranges of mountains and hills, and all of the people and inhabitants of the earth. Everyone was going about his or her daily routines totally unaware of what was about to happen.

Then, suddenly, everything changed. The sky turned dark with thick clouds and a deep sense of eeriness quickly overtook everything. With that darkness came a sudden and strange silence.

Almost immediately, the silence was broken by a deafeningly loud sound coming from Heaven. It was like seven claps of thunder rolled into one. Never had I heard such a sound in all of my life. It sounded like many trumpets, blasting so loudly that it not only pierced the ears of the men and women who heard it, but it resonated in their bones, as well. In response, their bodies shook with the terror that quickly took hold of them.

In the moments that followed, God allowed me to sense and feel what everyone else was sensing and feeling. When it happened, everybody reacted in much the same way—with a terrible, piercing scream. Men and women were filled with sudden terror, shock, fear, and helplessness such as they had never known before. They knew this was the end of time everyone had been talking about.

Next, it was as if someone had taken a razor blade and split the heavens, for here came the Lord Himself with all of His angels, and with Him came the power, glory, and majesty that only God could possess. Oh, such glory—and what beautiful colors! I thought of all of the different shades and palettes of colors I am so accustomed to seeing on the earth—all of the blues, greens, and yellows. But those colors I'd seen with my natural eyes in no way were comparable to the colors that were before me now! These were the supernatural colors of Heaven. Such majesty! Such power! Such glory!

As the Lord was breaking through the clouds and coming toward the earth, He was moving so rapidly that people couldn't think straight. It all happened so fast that I could easily understand why someone who thought it could never happen would be completely taken by surprise. I was seeing it all with my own eyes, and was in a state of disbelief, but it was happening exactly as the Lord said it would.

Many of those who saw the Lord were so frightened they urinated themselves and shook uncontrollably. There was total chaos and confusion. People were wailing, screaming, and didn't know what to do.

I will never forget when one young man cried out, "No! No! No! No! No! Wait! I thought I had time! I thought I had time! I thought I had time!"

Another cried out, "Oh, no! Wait! This must be a dream! This must be a dream! I will wake up! I will surely wake up!" But he couldn't wake up because he was already awake. It was not a dream—it was the real thing.

All around me people were screaming and running in confusion and terror. Then I heard a voice from Heaven saying, "This is the Day of the Lord, for it has come!"

Suddenly time stood still, and everything was about God. No one went to the malls to shop or to the theaters to see movies. No one was going about their business as usual. Now, for every soul on earth, time stood still, for the hour had come.

This was God's day, it was His hour, and somehow everyone knew it. People had often complained of frequently hearing the phrase, "Jesus is coming," or "Jesus is coming soon," but here it was. His coming had now become a reality. He had come and Earth's citizens were totally unprepared for His coming and what it meant for them.

By showing these events to me in advance, the Lord was commissioning me in a very special way to warn all mankind about the coming Day of the Lord. And the warning He showed me I must send echoing around the entire globe was this:

"I am coming!

I am coming!

I am coming!

Set your house in order!

Ready or not, here I come!"

When I came out of the vision, I was shaking uncontrollably. I always considered myself to be such a tough guy, but now I found myself curled up in the fetal position on the floor.

I began pleading for my life and soul. As tears poured from my eyes, I asked, "Please, God, allow me to be counted in that number." I prayed for the mercies of God upon my life and that I would be counted worthy to go with the Lord on the day that He comes. I already knew I was born again and would go to Heaven, but what I had just seen in the vision shook me to the very core of my being, leaving room for fear and doubt. The Lord catapulted me into the future to show me what is to come for humanity, and I didn't want anything to prevent me from being ready for it.

After I had prayed for myself, I earnestly prayed for my wife, my children, my mother, and my siblings. Then I began to intercede for preachers all over the world. In fact, I prayed two hours for preachers because they should be the voice of God in the earth today; they should be the ones who hold up the bloodstained banner. They are commissioned to preach the Gospel to all mankind. Only when the Lord released me did I stop praying.

A new anointing was now upon my life. I had been called to warn the nations, to declare that He is coming back whether we receive Him or not, and He is coming back whether we believe Him or not. Our Lord is coming soon. He commissioned me to declare it for Him and shout out, "I'm coming! I'm coming!"

He said to me very clearly, "I charge you now to warn all mankind that I'm coming, for the Day of the Lord is at hand."

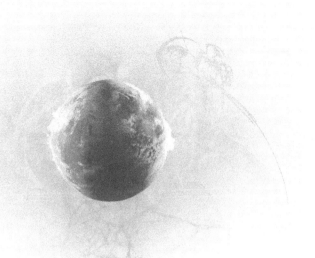

PART I

THE DAY OF
THE LORD

1

A SERIOUS CHANGE OF MINISTRY

I WAS A PASTOR FOR TEN YEARS BEFORE GOD CAME TO ME AND said, "I'm now sending you to the nations of the world, and I need you to move to Charlotte, North Carolina in order to spread the message of My coming."

Sid Roth, a mentor of mine, recently moved his entire ministry into the bustling town of Charlotte, North Carolina. I resigned from the church I was currently the pastor of in Katy, Texas, and my wife, Suzie, and I eventually found a suitable home for ourselves just over the border in South Carolina so we could be closer to Sid and his ministry.

For the first eight weeks, I didn't receive a single invitation to preach, and I began to get a little antsy. For many years, I had been preaching regularly every week and now I wasn't preaching at all. I called my friend, Kevin, and he comforted me.

"Well, Pastor David," he said, "you just stay in the will of God and things will work out. If God doesn't tell you anything in particular to do, then don't do anything. Just wait on Him." I knew Kevin was right.

I went to a church service and the pastor asked me to say a few words. After I delivered the message God had placed on my heart, the people began to rejoice and the pastor of the church was weeping and began to say, "The words you spoke were confirmation of what God has been speaking to our church." This was very encouraging to me. It is always exciting to see the Spirit of God ministering to His people. Toward the end of the service, an elderly prophetess of the church came up to me and said, "Man of God, God has you in a state of rest."

"He surely does," I agreed.

"God is going to download to you now," she continued, "and when you come out of this state of rest, your ministry will explode. God will send you out worldwide, but right now He has you resting. That's why the Scriptures say, *"Be still, and know that I am God: I will be exalted among the heathen, I will be exalted in the earth"* (Ps. 46:10).

It was one morning not long after this that the vision of the Day of the Lord came to me and my life was forever changed. In retrospect, it should not have come as a surprise. As I look back on it now, I see that God had already been dealing with me on this subject for many years.

MY FIRST CALL TO WARN OTHERS

Just a few years after I had given my heart to the Lord, He suddenly awoke me one morning. I looked at the clock and saw that it was just 5 a.m., and I sensed that the Lord wanted to talk to me about something. As I listened, I heard Him speak these words, "Go to the book of Ezekiel, the third chapter, and begin reading at the fourteenth verse." So, I reached for my Bible and opened it to that passage. I read:

> *So the spirit lifted me up, and took me away, and I went in bitterness, in the heat of my spirit; but the hand of the Lord*

was strong upon me. Then I came to them of the captivity at Telabib, that dwelt by the river of Chebar, and I sat where they sat, and remained there astonished among them seven days. And it came to pass at the end of seven days, that the word of the Lord came unto me, saying, **Son of man, I have made thee a watchman unto the house of Israel: therefore hear the word at my mouth, and give them warning from me.** *When I say unto the wicked, Thou shalt surely die; and thou givest him not warning, nor speakest to warn the wicked from his wicked way, to save his life; the same wicked man shall die in his iniquity; but his blood will I require at thine hand. Yet if thou warn the wicked, and he turn not from his wickedness, nor from his wicked way, he shall die in his iniquity; but thou hast delivered thy soul. Again, When a righteous man doth turn from his righteousness, and commit iniquity, and I lay a stumbling block before him, he shall die: because thou hast not given him warning, he shall die in his sin, and his righteousness which he hath done shall not be remembered; but his blood will I require at thine hand. Nevertheless if thou warn the righteous man, that the righteous sin not, and he doth not sin, he shall surely live, because he is warned; also thou hast delivered thy soul* (Ezekiel 3:14-21).

What would be the purpose of delivering such a warning to any man? It would be to save his life, to save his soul, to save him from himself, and to save him from the coming destruction. The response of the people wasn't Ezekiel's responsibility; being faithful to warn and declare all God revealed to him was what really mattered. At the end of the day, God was going to judge the people for their obedience or disobedience, but He was going to judge Ezekiel based on whether or not he was faithful to warn the people of the coming destruction. The name *Ezekiel* means "God strengthens." As Ezekiel was strengthened by God and instructed by Him to warn his contemporaries, I believe God was strengthening and instructing me to warn this generation to prepare for His eventual return. I knew that this is what God was calling me to do. When the full impact of it hit me, I fell out of the bed to my knees and began weeping and praying. I cried out, "Oh, my God, this is too great a responsibility!"

But God said, "You must carry My warning to the people whether they like it or not, whether they receive it or not, or whether they believe it or not." And that was that. God had placed His finger on my life in a new way, calling me to cry out and warn others about the coming Day of the Lord.

A PROPHETIC ANOINTING
FROM AN EARLY AGE

Let us ponder the story of Samuel the prophet, who at a very early age heard the voice of God.

And the child Samuel ministered unto the Lord before Eli. And the word of the Lord was precious in these days; there was no open vision; and it came to pass at that time, when Eli was laid down in his place, and his eyes began to wax dim, that he could not see. And ere the lamp of God went out in the temple of the Lord, where the ark of God was, and Samuel was laid down to sleep; that the Lord called Samuel: and he answered, Here am I. And he ran unto Eli, and said, Here am I; for thou calledst me. And he said, I called not; lie down again. And he went and lay down. And the lord called yet again, Samuel. And Samuel arose and went to Eli, and said, Here am I; for thou didst call me. And he answered, I called not, my son;

lie down again. Now Samuel did not yet know the Lord, neither was the word of the Lord yet revealed unto him. And the Lord called Samuel again the third time. And he arose and went to Eli, and said, Here am I; for thou didst call me. And Eli perceived that the Lord had called the child. Therefore Eli said unto Samuel, Go, lie down: and it shall be, if he call thee, that thou shalt say, Speak, Lord; for thy servant heareth. So Samuel went and lay down in his place. And the Lord came, and stood, and called as at other times, Samuel, Samuel. Then Samuel answered, Speak; for thy servant heareth. And the Lord said to Samuel, Behold, I will do a thing in Israel, at which both the ears of everyone that heareth it shall tingle. In that day I will perform against Eli all things which I have spoken concerning his house: when I begin, I will also make an end. For I told him that I will judge his house for ever for the iniquity which he knoweth; because his sons made themselves vile, and he restrained them not (1 Samuel 3:1-13).

This passage shows us that God spoke to Samuel at a very young age. This clearly demonstrates that age does not limit God's ability to use anyone. Ultimately, God can use all those who are willing to hear His voice and yield to His call, including children.

Many children possess the essential virtue of *humility*. Interestingly, in the book of Matthew Jesus addressed the importance of ensuring that adults, like little children, also *humble themselves* and adopt a child's perspective as it relates to their faith and trust in God.

And Jesus called a little child unto him, and set him in the midst of them, and said, Verily I say unto you, Except ye be converted, and become as little children, ye shall not enter into the kingdom of heaven. **Whosoever therefore shall humble himself as this little child, the same is greatest in the kingdom of heaven** (Matthew 18:2-4).

On this occasion Jesus was conveying a very powerful message. In essence, He was saying that we must all be converted and become as little children to enter the kingdom of Heaven. Children have a pure faith. Doubt and unbelief are generally not a part of their thinking as it relates to God. This is why God can use children to relay His message to humanity and why I believe God will use children like never before in these last days. Just as the Lord spoke to Samuel when he was a child and told him to warn Eli that God would judge his house, I believe God will also use our children to speak to many of us before He returns to earth.

One of the most unforgettable experiences of my life occurred when my son, Joshua, was only four years old. We were driving in the family car, and while he was sitting in the backseat he spoke out boldly, "Daddy, Daddy, when you are walking with Jesus don't look back! Don't look back!" Then he said it again with greater conviction, "Daddy, Daddy, when you are walking with Jesus don't look back! Don't look back!" When he was speaking these words his entire countenance changed. His demeanor became stern, serious, and authoritative. Then, when he had finished making his remark, he reverted to being a calm, fun-loving little boy and went back to looking out of the car window as though nothing happened. I am confident that what he said was a powerful message from God to me. As a result of this experience, I learned the importance of listening to our children, not only because we love them, but also because God may be attempting to speak to us through them in a much more profound and deeper way than we realize.

Similarly, as God used my son to speak to me, He also used me when I was a young boy to speak to one of my uncles. I hadn't realized it until later, but a prophetic anointing to warn others had actually been placed upon my life from the time I was only 11 years old.

During this time, my uncle Fred was staying with us. God used me to speak to him, even though at the time he was 28 and I was just eleven. Because we slept in the same room, we talked a lot. Most of our conversations were not significant, but one night it was different.

I remember how brightly the moon was shining through the window that night. Something sparked a memory in me, and so I said to him, "Uncle Fred, Grandma Minnie always taught me about God, even when I was very little. She told me that Jesus said unless we are born again, we couldn't hope to see Heaven. Instead, we'll die and go to hell and burn forever in the lake of fire and brimstone."

His reply was fairly typical of men who refuse to give God a place in their lives. "Junior," he said, "when you've got to go, you've got to go." It was the following Friday when I heard Grandma Louise calling him early in the morning to get up for work. I tried to wake him, only to find that he had died overnight. He'd been given one week's warning to prepare and to set his house in order before his time was up and God required his life from him.

God has said, *"To day if ye will hear his voice, harden not your hearts"* (Heb. 3:15). Because no one knows the day or the hour they will be gone, we should all live each day as though it were our last.

A WOMAN SAVED IN THE NICK OF TIME

Through the years I had other similar experiences. One Wednesday night, for example, I was teaching a Bible class, and I stopped in the middle of my message to say, "There's someone sitting in this church tonight, and this is your last call from God. He will not be coming to you ever again. This is your final call, so you must answer His call tonight."

Just then, a beautiful Hispanic girl with long black hair jumped up from the back and said, "It's me! I'm a backslider, and I want to come home." She was weeping before God, under conviction. We prayed for her that night, and she was restored to the Lord.

Two days later our daughter, Hannah, came home from school and told us about a terrible accident that had taken place. As the young Hispanic girl was leaving school that day, a carload of friends pulled up and invited her to go with them to McDonalds. They invited Hannah too, but a friend said to her, "I don't think your dad would like that." Thank God she declined. Hannah rode the school bus home, but the other girl got in the already crowded car with her friends.

The students on the bus could see the carload of kids in front of them. While the car moved toward the right-hand lane to make a turn, the driver decided to go around a car in front of them. As the driver made their move, a tractor trailer was coming at high speed from the opposite direction, and the car was hit head-on. It was a violent collision and pieces of the two vehicles flew wildly into the air.

Everyone saw what had happened and the school bus driver pulled over. Hannah ran to the car to try to help her friend. To her shock, she saw that the force of the accident had decapitated the young lady. A small child had also been catapulted from the car, and it took the police 48 hours to locate the child's body. In all, eight people died that day. The only person to survive the accident was the driver, and she was never the same again. She suffered a complete emotional collapse.

Who knows whether the other young people in that car had also been warned, but fortunately the young lady had been warned by God and had set her house in order just two days before. Thank God she had come forward and rededicated her life to Him in time. As a result, at least one soul was saved.

PREPARING TO BATTLE COMPLACENCY

Even as I accepted this new calling, I sensed that I would be battling the complacency of our time. Because of all the talk of Jesus's coming through the years without Him actually coming, people have become complacent and lax about their spiritual welfare. But everything He said must come to pass at some point in time. Isaiah declared, *"So shall my word be that goeth forth out of my mouth: it shall not return unto me void, but it shall accomplish that which I please, and it shall prosper in the thing whereto I sent it"* (Isa. 55:11). We know Isaiah was speaking for God, so it is sure to come to pass, and it will be sooner than any of us expects.

One of the weapons to battle complacency is the fear of the Lord. But where is the fear of God today? We don't hear it preached much in many churches today, and it's a subject people are often uncomfortable with. The Bible teaches that the fear of God is foundational to our walk with Him.

The fear of the Lord is a fountain of life (Proverb 14:27).

The fear of the Lord is the beginning of wisdom: a good understanding have all they that do his commandments (Psalm 111:10).

The fear of the Lord is the beginning of knowledge: but fools despise wisdom and instruction (Proverb 1:7).

The fear of the Lord is the beginning of wisdom: and the knowledge of the holy is understanding (Proverb 9:10).

Only fools despise such warnings. They say, "Who do you think you are? I don't want to hear that. We've been doing just fine without you. We've been having a good time." But the Bible warns us to obey God, not man, and the time is here to declare the Day of the Lord, because it is at hand—it is nearer than ever before. Consequently, I am going to obey God and warn the world to prepare for His second coming.

As I came out of the vision that day, the Lord said to me again, "I charge you now to warn all of mankind, to warn them of the Day of the Lord, to warn them that I'm coming in an hour and at a time when they least expect it." There could be no doubt—this was my charge.

The fear of the Lord is the beginning of wisdom and knowledge.

God is greatly to be feared in the assembly of the saints (Psalm 89:7).

Fear not them which kill the body, but are not able to kill the soul: but rather fear him which is able to destroy both soul and body in hell (Matthew 10:28).

We should all truly love God, fear God, and be prepared to meet Him when our time comes to leave this earth and stand before Him to give an account. We never really know when our time will come to leave this life. Let's make sure we're ready!

PUTTING THE CALL INTO ACTION

After my time of rest was up subsequent to my move to South Carolina, I was invited to do a one-week revival in Baton Rouge, Louisiana. It was there that I began to preach this message, to declare that He is coming *"as a thief in the night"* (1 Thess. 5:2), that no one knows the day or the hour when the Lord will come (Matt. 24:36)—but He *will* come. Nothing that we can do will change the fact of His coming. Jesus says in His Word, *"For verily I say unto you, Till heaven and earth pass, one jot or one tittle shall in no wise pass from the law, till all be fulfilled"* (Matt. 5:18)—*all* will be fulfilled!

During that first week of meetings in Baton Rouge, revival broke out. People were being healed where they stood. They ran to the altar, screaming and wailing. They were crying out to God, "Save us, Lord! Save us! Forgive us of our sins! Forgive us of our trespasses!" This cry came from the entire church, including the pastor and his wife. Everyone was under the strongest conviction I had ever seen. I, too, fell to my knees and began weeping and thanking God.

This went on for 21 days. I preached every night and twice on Sundays. During my visit, I also spoke on the radio to a wider audience. As people in the area heard what God was doing, more began to come to the church. Among them were pastors, prophets, evangelists, and teachers. They sensed the urgency I felt in my spirit, and they responded. One pastor said to me, "I want to put you on my radio program for a whole month," and he played my teaching CDs on-air.

During the weeks that followed, as I preached in other places around the country large numbers of Christians came running and screaming to the altars. Many were backsliders and doing things they knew were not right, and they recognized that it was God who had put this warning upon my lips. In this way, God was giving them another chance. Others realized that, for one reason or another, their readiness for His coming had been compromised, and they wanted to repair their relationship with Him. I sensed that many were like those I had seen in my vision who cried out, "No! Wait! I thought I had time!" or "Oh, no! Wait! This must be a dream! I will surely wake up!" They were unprepared.

I marveled at the fact that God was using me in this way to warn His people. When He said to me, "I charge you to warn all mankind," I reminded Him that I am nothing but a hunk of flesh. It always amazes me how God will use imperfect beings to help perfect the rest of us. He said in His Word that He gave the five-fold ministry in order to bring the Church to maturity:

> And he gave some, **apostles**; and some, **prophets**; and some, **evangelists**; and some, **pastors and teachers**; for the perfecting of the saints, for the work of the ministry, for the edifying of the body of Christ: till we all come in the unity of the faith, and of the knowledge of the Son of God, unto a perfect man, unto the measure of the stature of the fulness of Christ: that we henceforth be no more children, tossed to and fro, and carried about with every wind of doctrine, by the sleight of men, and cunning craftiness, whereby they lie in wait to deceive; but speaking the truth in love, may grow up into him in all things, which is the head, even Christ: from whom the whole body fitly joined

together and compacted by that which every joint supplieth, according to the effectual working in the measure of every part, maketh increase of the body unto the edifying of itself in love (Ephesians 4:11-16).

Why did God place these ministries (performed by humble men and women) in the church? It was *"for the perfecting of the saints, for the work of the ministry, for the edifying of the body of Christ"* (Eph. 4:12). Each of us has a certain ministry to perform, and we will each have to answer to God for what we have done with that gift. What have you done with the talents God has given you? As for me, I knew that I must be faithful to cry aloud and spare not, warning everyone God gave me an audience with of the coming Day of the Lord.

One preacher said to me, "I was so hardheaded that I was running from God, and I overdosed on cocaine and died and went to hell. While I was there in hell, God spoke to me and said, 'What have you done with the life I have given you?' I said, 'God, if You will just give me another chance, if You will just get me out of this terrible place, I will serve You all the days of my life.'" God brought that brother back from the dead, and he's been serving Him ever since. He now pastors a large church that's on fire for God. When he preaches, it is with strong conviction, because he's been to hell and knows firsthand what it's like.

WHY I CARRY THIS MESSAGE

There's a reason I can carry this message so close to my heart and am so passionate about warning others of the coming judgment. Over the years I have learned to take correction from God. If we don't learn how to receive correction from Him, God describes us as "bastards," not sons. The writer of Hebrews states:

> *And ye have forgotten the exhortation which speaketh unto you as unto children, My son, despise not thou the chastening of the Lord, nor faint when thou art rebuked of him: for whom the Lord loveth he chasteneth, and scourgeth every son whom he receiveth. If ye endure chastening, God dealeth with you as with sons; for what son is he whom the father chasteneth not?* ***But if ye be without chastisement, whereof all are partakers, then are ye bastards, and not sons*** (Hebrews 12:5-8).

If a person can't take rebuke or correction, they're certainly not authorized to preach it or teach it to others. The Scriptures advise us, *"Open rebuke is better than secret love"* (Prov. 27:5). Receive God's rebuke today and you will be spared on the Day of the Lord. Not only that, but you will also be qualified to warn others.

Please don't resent these words. People who are truly your best friends will always tell you the truth. You might invite them over for a meal, and while you're sitting at the table eating together they might say, "You know you were wrong." Then, just as quickly, they might continue, "Now pass me a chicken leg," or "Give me some of those delicious biscuits and gravy." That's what a true friend does. Never buddy up with people who will only tell you what you want to hear. That's not the way to get delivered and set free from fleshly things that can prevent you from having God's best for your life.

Jesus said, *"Ye shall know the truth, and the truth shall make you free"* (John 8:32). There are a lot of people sitting in church pews today who desperately want to be free, but they don't know how to gain the freedom they so desperately desire. Here is the secret we've all been looking for: the truth of the Word of God has the power to make you free. Believe it and apply it today.

Because time is so short and the coming of the Day of the Lord is at hand, God is looking for men and women to stand in the gap, to intercede for people to turn to Him. He said through the prophet Ezekiel, *"And I sought for a man among them, that should make up the hedge, and stand in the gap before me for the land, that I should not destroy it: but I found none"* (Ezek. 22:30). Can God count on you to stand in the gap?

In much the same way, He called Isaiah. When Isaiah went into the temple, he saw the glory of the Lord—he heard His voice and experienced His power. As the doorposts of the temple shook at His voice, Isaiah saw his own humanity and cried out, *"Woe is me! for I am undone; because I am a man of unclean lips, and I dwell in the midst of a people of unclean lips: for mine eyes have seen the King, the Lord of hosts"* (Isa. 6:5).

In response to this, the Lord sent an angel to touch Isaiah's lips and cleanse him. When this was accomplished, the Lord asked, *"Whom shall I send, and who will go for us?"* Isaiah answered, *"Here am I; send me"* (Isa. 6:8). In exactly the same way, I felt compelled to answer God's call on my life by saying, "I'll preach this message whether people love me or not; I'll preach it whether they bless me or not; I'll preach it whether they receive me or not. I must, for souls are hanging in the balance, and You have commissioned me to do this work."

God called me to change my ministry and to begin focusing on warning others of the approaching Day of the Lord. The vision changed my life forever and solidified in my heart the certainty of the days that lie ahead.

2

THE ABSOLUTE CERTAINTY OF THESE THINGS

WHAT GOD TELLS US IN HIS WORD IS SURER THAN ANY element of our daily life. He has declared that not one part of His Word will go unfulfilled, even if Heaven and earth should pass away. *"I tell you the truth, until heaven and earth disappear, not even the smallest detail of God's law will disappear until its purpose is achieved"* (Matt. 5:18 NLT).

Everything God spoke throughout His Word is absolutely certain to come to pass. You can count on it and should get ready for it. This doesn't mean focusing only on the the parts we like and the parts that make us feel good.

Have you perhaps allowed someone to convince you that Jesus will not come back again or that He will delay His coming? Have you even been deceived into believing that there is no hell, no place of torment, and no end of time? Well, a certain rich man Jesus taught about experienced it, and we can read about his experience in detail.

THE RICH MAN AND LAZARUS

In Luke 16:19-31, the Bible tells of two men; one of them was a rich man who *"fared sumptuously every day"* and was *"clothed in purple and fine linen"* (Luke 16:19), and the other was a beggar named Lazarus who was laid daily at the rich man's gate, begging for food. Lazarus had sunk so low financially that he even sought the crumbs that fell from the rich man's table.

The Bible describes the beggar as having sores all over his body that the dogs came and licked (see Luke 16:20). I'm sure it was not a pretty sight! This poor man was clearly suffering and hungry, but the rich man could not have cared less about his welfare.

The rich man died, and he was tormented in the flames of hell. Lazarus also died, but immediately he was in the bosom of Abraham. The rich man was able to see the beggar he had rejected in Abraham's presence, and he cried out, "Father Abraham, will you have Lazarus come dip his finger in a cup of water and touch my tongue because I'm tormented in these flames?" (see Luke 16:24). The man was clearly accustomed to giving orders and having them obeyed, but this time it would be different.

Abraham told him that he couldn't, because there was a great gulf between them and they couldn't pass it (see Luke 16:26). The man pleaded, "Well, then, at least have him go back and warn my brothers not to come to this place" (see Luke 16:27-28).

This wish could also not be met, and Abraham answered, *"They have Moses and the prophets; let them hear them"* (Luke 16:29). The rich man insisted that if someone were to go back from the dead, surely they would believe then (see Luke 16:30). But Abraham said, "Even if one came back from the dead, they will not believe him" (see Luke 16:31). What a sad commentary on the state of some members of humanity as reflected by the rich man's siblings!

In that moment, if this man could have done it all over again, he would have done things very differently. But that's not the way it works. Only God gets to decide if we have more time. When He says time is up, there is no going back.

For this rich man it was too late. You and I never know when it might be too late for us as well. Therefore, we must maintain a tender, forgiving, and generous heart on a daily basis, for we just don't know when our hour of reckoning will come. *"And as it is appointed unto men once to die, but after this the judgment"* (Heb. 9:27).

People have asked me how it is that I know time is running out and that all of these events will happen soon. I can't tell you exactly how I know, but all I can say is that I just know. Furthermore, I know that it is my responsibility to warn the nations of it before it is too late.

Can I convince them before time runs out? Maybe. Maybe not. But that's not my responsibility. All I can do is warn them, being faithful to God's calling over my life.

This is not just a message for non-Christians; many Christians are also not ready for the coming Day of the Lord. Some say, "Well I've been saved for 30 years already. I've been going to church all of my life." Really? Jesus said, *"This people draweth nigh unto me with their mouth, and honoureth me with their lips; but their heart is far from me"* (Matt. 15:8). If that describes you, then this is your warning. Receive it humbly and act on it today.

WHEN YOU'VE DONE IT TO THE LEAST OF THESE, YOU'VE DONE IT UNTO ME

Jesus is coming back in all of His glory and will gather all the nations of the earth and separate its inhabitants into two very distinct groups. Once separated, one group will inherit the Kingdom of God, the other will be cast into everlasting fire. With our choices we will all have the opportunity to ultimately choose what group we will belong to. If we are going to eventually form part of the right group of individuals welcomed by God into Heaven, we will need to make sure that one of the things we do well while alive is to live a life of service and sacrifice to God and to our fellow human beings.

The Lord Jesus spent time teaching His followers a very profound lesson regarding the responsibility that they and we all have to truly live what we know to be true about how we are to treat others.

> *When the Son of man shall come in his glory, and all the holy angels with him, then shall he sit upon the throne of his glory: and before him shall be gathered all nations: and he shall separate them one from another, as a shepherd divideth his sheep from the goats: and he shall set the sheep on his right hand, but the goats on the left. Then shall the King say unto them on his right hand, Come, ye blessed of my Father, inherit the kingdom prepared for you from the foundation of the world: for I was an hungred, and ye gave me meat: I was thirsty, and ye gave me drink: I was a stranger, and ye took me in: naked, and ye clothed me: I was sick, and ye visited me: I was in prison, and ye came unto me. Then shall the righteous answer him, saying, Lord, when saw we thee an hungred, and fed*

thee? or thirsty, and gave thee drink? When saw we thee a stranger, and took thee in? or naked, and clothed thee? Or when saw we thee sick, or in prison, and came unto thee? And the King shall answer and say unto them, Verily I say unto you, Inasmuch as ye have done it unto one of the least of these my brethren, ye have done it unto me. Then shall he say also unto them on the left hand, Depart from me, ye cursed, into everlasting fire, prepared for the devil and his angels: for I was an hungred, and ye gave me no meat: I was thirsty, and ye gave me no drink: I was a stranger, and ye took me not in: naked, and ye clothed me not: sick, and in prison, and ye visited me not. Then shall they also answer him, saying, Lord, when saw we thee an hungred, or athirst, or a stranger, or naked, or sick, or in prison, and did not minister unto thee? Then shall he answer them, saying, Verily I say unto you, Inasmuch as ye did it not to one of the least of these, ye did it not to me. And these shall go away into everlasting punishment: but the righteous into life eternal (Matthew 25:31-46).

This passage asks the following questions: If we are saved by the grace of God and not by works, why did Jesus say that so many who neglected to do certain works would be cast into everlasting fire? Why did He say that so many would go to this horrible place of torment as a result of not what they did but what they failed to do? Maybe it is because there are not only sins of commission, but also sins of omission. We sin not only by what we do, but also by what we fail to do. The Bible says, *"Therefore to him that knoweth to do good, and doeth it not, to him it is sin"* (James 4:17).

God's Word tells us that, *"by grace are ye saved through faith; and that not of yourselves: it is the gift of God: not of works, lest any man should boast"* (Eph. 2:8-9). Thus, we are saved by *"grace"* through *"faith."* However, we cannot make it to Heaven on grace that is animated by *"dead faith."* To avoid "dead faith," we must understand what genuine faith truly is. We know that faith is defined as follows: *"faith is the substance of things hoped for, the evidence of things not seen"* (Heb. 11:1). Now that we know what true faith is, we should also learn what false or dead faith is. James explains "dead faith" as follows: *"For as the body without the spirit is dead, so faith without works is dead also"* (James 2:26). Because faith without works is dead, then dead faith is one unsupported by actions that evidence its existence. For faith to be meaningful, good works must accompany it. Why is it that good works make faith real and consequential? Because if people truly believe in something, they will live it! If they don't, they will be pretenders or hypocrites trying to masquerade as the real thing. Actions truly speak louder than words! James wrote, *"Yea, a man may say, Thou hast faith, and I have works: shew me thy faith without thy works, and I will shew thee my faith by my works"* (James 2:18).

Thus we've learned that it is by what we do and not only by what we say that we show our love for God and others. Do your actions demonstrate your love for God? Do your actions demonstrate your love for your neighbor?

One thing I've learned about the love of God is that true love always *gives*. True love always does something. Love is an action word. *"For God so loved the world, that he gave his only begotten Son, that whosoever believeth in him should not perish, but have everlasting life"* (John 3:16). God demonstrated His love toward us by *giving* His only begotten son to die for us so that He could redeem us from destruction. *"But God commendeth his love toward us, in that, while we were yet sinners, Christ died for us"* (Rom. 5:8). God *did* something to show us how much He loved us. He *gave* His one and only divinely conceived Son, Jesus Christ, to save our souls so that He could secure for us everlasting life.

There is great wisdom in following Jesus's example of loving by giving. When we refuse to show our love for others by giving of our time, talents, and resources, we end up deceiving ourselves. The Scripture says, *"But be ye doers of the word, and not hearers only, deceiving your own selves"* (James 1:22). We say we love others, but many of us do little or nothing to show it. John encourages us to *"not love in word, neither in tongue; but in deed and in truth"* (1 John 3:18). This is the kind of love God wants us to engage in. The Word reminds us that, *"whoso hath this world's good, and seeth his brother have need, and shutteth up his bowels of compassion from him, how dwelleth the love of God in him?"* (1 John 3:17). Can you see? Love combined with action is real, palpable, and truly meaningful in the sight of God and man. Love without action is, in the end, meaningless and powerless.

The foregoing message contained in the Bible became real to me years ago. Shortly after I had started a church, I remember that when it came time to receive offerings for the ministry, many church members were giving very little of their resources to the work of the Lord. I knew that if God did not have their money, He did not have their hearts. *"For where your treasure is, there will your heart be also"* (Matt. 6:21). So the Lord directed me to teach the people on the subject of giving, and specifically on the topic of ensuring that their giving was done *"as to the Lord, and not unto men"* (Col. 3:23). Then I taught them about the "Principle of Sowing and Reaping," and they began to understand more and more about the power of loving through giving. This changed their mindset. They began to show their love for God's work and learned to give more and, consequently, to receive more. The blessings in their lives increased dramatically. *"Be not deceived; God is not mocked: for whatsoever a man soweth, that shall he also reap"* (Gal. 6:7).

The "Principle of Sowing and Reaping" is very powerful. On numerous occasions I have personally experienced its benefits. One of those occasions occurred when I was pastoring a church. I remember that at the time I did not have a car and I would have to walk to church every service. When I was walking to church one day, an elderly church member saw me walking and offered to give me a ride. As we were driving toward our destination, she said, "Pastor, you shouldn't have to walk to church." The next thing I knew, she went out and bought me a car. It was a '98 Oldsmobile that she eventually had titled to my name. I was so excited. I kept thanking her for the great blessing she had bestowed upon my life.

After receiving the car, I quickly jumped inside to give it a test drive. While I was driving, God spoke to me and said, "Give the car away." I said, "Oh, Lord, but I just got the car." Then I paused briefly, thought about it, and said in surrender, "Nevertheless, I will give it away as You have asked." Then I asked Him, "Lord, who do You want me to give the car to?" The Lord told me to give the car to a Christian man in our church who was a single parent to eight children. He didn't have a car, and his entire family had to walk to church every service. In obedience, I went straight to this man's home to give him the car. I knew that delayed obedience would be considered disobedience. As soon as I arrived at the man's home, in disbelief he said, "Is that mine, Pastor?" I said, "Yes, brother, here's the title to the car." I handed him the title and he began to cry and kept thanking me for the car. I said to him, "I have one question— can you give me a ride home?" He gladly agreed to my request and drove me home.

It was difficult to obey God, but I knew that I had done the right thing. About two weeks later, unbeknownst to me one of the other church members bought me a brand new Ford pick-up truck. It was royal blue and it was exactly what I had been wanting. I really needed a car, and this one was not only new, but it was also completely paid for. I was so excited. God had blessed me greatly. I believe with all my heart that this would not have happened if I had not obeyed Him when He spoke to me. That act of obedience is what released the blessing and placed the "Principle of Sowing and Reaping" into motion. This built my faith and showed me that, in some way, I was blessing Jesus as well and I was being true to His words when He said, *"Inasmuch as ye have done it unto one of the least of these my brethren, ye have done it unto me"* (Matt. 25:40). This was encouraging because I, like many of you, desire to hear Jesus say to me on the day I stand before Him to give an account, *"Well done, thou good and faithful servant"* (Matt. 25:21).

WHAT JESUS TAUGHT ABOUT BEING READY

Many of the teachings of Jesus are related to this subject of being ready for His coming. He also taught many parables with the same theme. Here's just one that relates to being ready and watchful for the coming of the Lord:

> *Let your loins be girded about, and your lights burning; and ye yourselves like unto men that wait for their lord, when he will return from the wedding; that when he cometh and knocketh, they may open unto him immediately. Blessed are*

those servants, whom the lord when he cometh shall find watching: verily I say unto you, that he shall gird himself, and make them to sit down to meat, and will come forth and serve them. And if he shall come in the second watch, or come in the third watch, and find them so, blessed are those servants. And this know, that if the goodman of the house had known what hour the thief would come, he would have watched, and not have suffered his house to be broken through. **Be ye therefore ready also: for the Son of man cometh at an hour when ye think not.**

Then Peter said unto him, Lord, speakest thou this parable unto us, or even to all?

And the Lord said, Who then is that faithful and wise steward, whom his lord shall make ruler over his household, to give them their portion of meat in due season? Blessed is that servant, whom his lord when he cometh shall find so doing. Of a truth I say unto you, that he will make him ruler over all that he hath. But and if that servant say in his heart, My lord delayeth his coming; and shall begin to beat the menservants and maidens, and to eat and drink, and to be drunken; the lord of that servant will come in a day when he looketh not for him, and at an hour when he is not aware, and will cut him in sunder, and will appoint him his portion with the unbelievers. **And that servant, which knew his lord's will, and prepared not himself, neither did according to his will, shall be beaten with many stripes.** *But he that knew not, and did commit things worthy of stripes, shall be beaten with few stripes. For unto whomsoever much is given, of him shall be much required: and to whom men have committed much, of him they will ask the more* (Luke 12:35-48).

Notice what will befall a servant who knows his lord's will but does not prepare himself for his coming: he shall be punished. Ignorance is no excuse, but those who are ignorant will suffer a less severe punishment than those who know what's right and do it not. Now, we all have been duly warned, so we have absolutely no excuse when the Day comes for us to stand before the Lord.

We should fear the Lord and heed His words. Remember what Mary said about Him, *"And his mercy is on them that fear him from generation to generation"* (Luke 1:50). Further, Jesus taught, *"And fear not them which kill the body, but are not able to kill the soul: but rather fear him which is able to destroy both soul and body in hell"* (Matt. 10:28). For those who don't fear God, all bets are off.

WATCH AND PRAY

Jesus told His disciples that Heaven and earth would eventually pass away, but what would abide forever would be His words. God's Words are true, powerful, and eternal!

God's eternal word teaches us that no one knows the exact day or the exact hour when Jesus will return. Thus Jesus, while on earth, cautioned His disciples not to *sleep* or *slumber*, but to *watch* and *pray*.

> *Heaven and earth shall pass away: but my words shall not pass away. But of that day and that hour knoweth no man, no, not the angels which are in heaven, neither the Son, but the Father. Take ye heed,* **watch and pray:** *for ye know not when the time is. For the Son of Man is as a man taking a far journey, who left his house, and gave authority to his servants, and to every man his work, and commanded the porter to watch.* **Watch ye therefore:** *for*

*ye know not when the master of the house cometh, at even,
or at midnight, or at the cockcrowing, or in the morning:
lest coming suddenly he find you **sleeping**. And what I say
unto you I say unto all, **Watch*** (Mark 13:31-37).

The Lord knew that throughout life many people would be
tempted to be lackadaisical in their approach to spiritual issues.
He knew that there would be a natural tendency, on the part
of some, to become spiritually sluggish and yield to the desires
of the flesh. He knew that this laid-back, unconcerned attitude
would result in numerous souls not being ready for His return.
His desire, however, is that all would be prepared and ready for
His second coming. An example of this tendency to be spiritually
lax occurred just before Jesus was to be beaten and crucified by
the Romans. Prior to Jesus going to the Garden of Gethsemane
to pray, He told his disciples: *"My soul is exceeding sorrowful, even
unto death: tarry ye here, and watch with me"* (Matt. 26:38). Then
Jesus went a little further and fell on His face and prayed to God
that the cup of suffering that He was about to partake of would
pass from Him. The prospect of what He was soon to experience
was overwhelming. He wanted to be spared the pain. Nonethe-
less, immediately after Jesus had spoken these words, He said with
a great sense of conviction, *"nevertheless not as I will, but as thou
wilt"* (Matt. 26:39). Jesus had made a conscious choice that the
will of God would be paramount in His life. Jesus was truly Holy
Spirit-led. He was committed to ensuring that His flesh was not
going to get in the way of accomplishing the will of God for His
life. He was determined to completely and totally submit His will
to God's will. From His perspective, the Old Testament prophe-
cies with respect to His death, burial, and resurrection were going
to be fulfilled regardless of how He felt in the natural. Jesus said,

"For I came down from heaven, not to do mine own will, but the will of him that sent me" (John 6:38).

The question then became, would Jesus's disciples also have the spiritual maturity necessary to make the same choice that Jesus made to submit His will to God's will? The Bible tells us that after Jesus prayed, He returned to look for His disciples and found them *sleeping.* He asked Peter, *"What, could ye not watch with me one hour?"* (Matt. 26:40). All that Jesus asked them to do was to pray for a short period of time, yet they did not accede to His request. They instead yielded to their flesh and not to the Spirit. Then Jesus cautioned them, *"Watch and pray, that ye enter not into temptation: the spirit indeed is willing, but the flesh is weak"* (Matt. 26:41).

We must heed this warning. We must watch and we must pray if Jesus is to find us ready when He returns. We must subjugate our flesh to the authority of God's Word. Paul the apostle was very much aware of the dangers of not subjugating his flesh and wrote, *"But I keep under my body, and bring it into subjection: lest that by any means, when I have preached to others, I myself should be a castaway"* (1 Cor. 9:27). Paul knew how weak his flesh was and understood the battle between the flesh and the spirit. In his epistle to the Galatians he explained: *"For the flesh lusteth against the Spirit, and the Spirit against the flesh: and these are contrary the one to the other: so that ye cannot do the things that ye would"* (Gal. 5:17). This is why he was so committed to ensuring that his flesh was fully submitted to the will of God. He did not want to become a castaway. Do you want to become a castaway? If not, then follow Paul's example and bring your flesh under subjection to the will of God. Paul understood the perils of the flesh and said, *"For I know that in me (that is, in my flesh,) dwelleth no good thing"* (Romans 7:18).

Paul also highlighted some other important truths that are relevant to the subject at hand when he wrote an epistle to the Thessalonians and warned them to *"Quench not the Spirit"* (1 Thess. 5:19) and to *"Pray without ceasing"* (1 Thess. 5:17). You see, God has called us to pray at all times because: *Prayer changes things! Prayer is powerful! Prayer is effective!* And we know with certainty that *"The effectual fervent prayer of a righteous man availeth much"* (James 5:16). Jesus Himself conveyed this same message during His ministry to others on earth. By example, He underscored the importance of having a consistent prayer life. He always made time to get alone with God and seek His face. He knew where His strength came from. Moreover, He spoke a parable to His disciples in which He delivered this powerful message. *"And he spake a parable unto them to this end, that men ought always to pray, and not to faint"* (Luke 18:1).

Remaining humble, forsaking our own selfish ways, and seeking God through prayer should be viewed by all as a fundamental part of life. Seeking God consistently and unfailingly is part and parcel of the Christian experience. God desires that we turn away from all things that in the grand scheme of things are unimportant and insignificant and that we seek Him diligently. We cannot allow the good in our lives to become the enemy of the great. We also cannot permit any kind of evil to thwart our objective of seeking the Lord regularly. Isaiah said to God's people, *"Seek ye the Lord while he may be found, call ye upon him while he is near: let the wicked forsake his way, and the unrighteous man his thoughts: and let him return unto the Lord, and he will have mercy upon him; and to our God, for he will abundantly pardon"* (Isa.

55:6-7). In the New Testament, James told believers, *"Draw nigh to God, and he will draw nigh to you"* (James 4:8). He went on to say, *"Cleanse your hands, ye sinners; and purify your hearts, ye double minded"* (James 4:8). It is time to purify ourselves. It is time to touch not the unclean thing and to come to the Lord with clean hands and a grateful heart. In Jeremiah, the Lord said to His people, *"And ye shall seek me, and find me, when ye shall search for me with all your heart"* (Jer. 29:13). It is when we seek God with all our hearts that we will assuredly find Him.

God calls on us to purify our hearts and be single-minded in our approach to serving Him. All throughout the Bible we find examples of the Lord forgiving and receiving those who seek Him, are repentant in heart, and are clothed with an attitude of humility and godly sorrow. The book of Second Chronicles documents God charging Solomon one night, *"If my people, which are called by my name, shall **humble themselves, and pray, and seek my face, and turn from their wicked ways;** then will I hear from heaven, and will forgive their sin, and will heal their land"* (2 Chron. 7:14) In this passage we are afforded unique insight into God's desire to forgive sin, to shower grace and mercy on those who turn from their wicked ways, and to receive the contrite in heart unto Himself. One of the most important components accompanying true repentance is a sincere attitude of humility. For we know that *"God resisteth the proud, but giveth grace unto the humble"* (James 4:6). Let us rid ourselves of pride and embrace humility in all that we say and do.

From time to time, engaging in a little introspection and self-examination can be very helpful. The apostle Paul wrote, *"Examine yourselves, whether ye be in the faith; prove your own selves. Know ye not your own selves, how that Jesus Christ is in you, except ye be reprobates?"* (2 Cor. 13:5). On occasion we need to ask ourselves if our actions are following our faith. Are we truly living what we believe to be true and right in the eyes of God? Do we hunger and thirst for the things of the Spirit of God? Do we desire to be in His presence more than anything else in the world? We should always be hungering and thirsting for God's company, even as King David did. For he wrote passionately, *"As the hart panteth after the water brooks, so panteth my soul after thee, O God. My soul thirsteth for God, for the living God: when shall I come and appear before God?"* (Ps. 42:1-2). His soul yearned to be in God's presence. He said of the Lord, *"in thy presence is fulness of joy; at thy right hand there are pleasures for evermore"* (Ps. 16:11). I encourage you to seek the Lord diligently, for He *"is a rewarder of them that diligently seek him"* (Heb. 11:6). We know that ultimately our greatest reward is the Lord Himself!

BE WISE, DON'T BE FOOLISH

When will your time be up? No one knows but God. Thus, you should be wise and not foolish. Pray, seek God, be spiritually ready at all times to meet the Lord. Your time may come when you least expect it. Jesus told a parable of ten virgins; five of them were wise and five were foolish. The five wise virgins were ready for the bridegroom's return; the five foolish ones were not. What did the wise virgins do differently than the foolish ones? Let us read and find out.

> *Then shall the kingdom of heaven be likened unto ten virgins, which took their lamps, and went forth to meet the bridegroom. And five of them were wise, and five were foolish. They that were foolish took their lamps, and took no oil with them: but the wise took oil in their vessels with*

their lamps. While the bridegroom tarried, they all slum-
bered and slept. And at midnight there was a cry made,
Behold, the bridegroom cometh; go ye out to meet him.
Then all those virgins arose, and trimmed their lamps.
And the foolish said unto the wise, Give us of your oil; for
our lamps are gone out. But the wise answered, saying,
Not so; lest there be not enough for us and you: but go ye
rather to them that sell, and buy for yourselves. And while
they went to buy, the bridegroom came; **and they that**
were ready went in with him to the marriage: and the
door was shut. *Afterward came also the other virgins,*
saying, Lord, Lord, open to us. But he answered and said,
Verily I say unto you, I know you not. **Watch therefore,**
for ye know neither the day nor the hour wherein the
Son of man cometh (Matthew 25:1-13).

Jesus is the bridegroom and He is coming back for His bride, the Church. The Church is the true body of believers who have been saved and washed clean by the blood of Jesus, who is *"the Lamb of God, which taketh away the sin of the world"* (John 1:29).

In the passage above, Jesus tells us that the foolish virgins did not take oil with them. They were not prepared to meet the bridegroom. They had not been doing the things that were necessary to be ready. As a result, they missed the marriage. Additionally, because they were not ready, when the time came to go into the marriage, the foolish virgins came to the wise and asked them to give them some of the oil in their lamps. The response given was, *"Not so; lest there be not enough for us and you: but go ye rather to them that sell, and buy for yourselves. And while they went to buy, the bridegroom came; and they that were ready went in with him to the marriage: and the door was shut"* (Matt. 25:9-10). Salvation is not transferable; you are either prepared for Lord's return because you have been praying, fasting, reading His word, and walking with Him daily, or you are not. There is no in-between!

Today there are many who mistakenly say that they are too busy and don't have time to pray and seek God. They say that they have other, more important, things to do than to spend time with God. However, the truth is that all of us don't have time to do anything; instead we intentionally make time to do the things we truly want to do. Whether we realize it or not, the things we do are what we consider genuine priorities in our lives. So what are your priorities? Just evaluate what it is you spend time doing and you will find out that these activities are your true priorities. Truth be told, it is not *what you say* but *what you do* that defines who you really are. What *you do* shows what you truly value and think is important in life. Is God important to your life? How much time do you spend with Him? True believers live the word and seek God diligently; false believers don't. This is why James admonished Jesus's followers so authoritatively when he wrote, *"But be ye doers of the word, and not hearers only, deceiving your own selves"* (James 1:22). Be real! Live the Word!

When we claim to have faith in God but then allow our actions to contradict our words, we deceive ourselves. We end up behaving hypocritically and we lie to ourselves. At times, both consciously and subconsciously we find ourselves trying to find some sort of justification for neglecting to seek God. We get very creative when making excuses as to why we don't have the time for God or His Kingdom. When will seeking God and putting Him first become a priority in our lives? Memorably, one of Jesus's disciples tried to make an excuse as to why he could not follow Jesus when he was asked to do so. He said, *"Lord, suffer me first to go and bury my father"* (Matt. 8:21). Jesus responded, *"Follow me;*

and let the dead bury their dead" (Matt. 8:22). In other words, as good as that excuse may have sounded, it was meaningless as it related to the more important issue of following Christ. Jesus made it clear that not even family should be placed above Him in terms of our priorities. Jesus said, *"He that loveth father or mother more than me is not worthy of me: and he that loveth son or daughter more than me is not worthy of me"* (Matt. 10:37). Nothing and no one should take precedence over Christ.

Who or what are we placing before God? Is it our father, our mother, our children, or our best friend? Is it our car, our home, or other material possessions that we are secretly idolizing? Is it sporting events or other activities that we are placing first? There are many great blessings God has bestowed upon our lives; let's not place those blessings before God, lest they become stumbling blocks in our path.

Followers of Christ must remain true to their identity as obedient servants of the Most High, and they must obey His word unconditionally. For we know that *"if any be a hearer of the word, and not a doer, he is like unto a man beholding his natural face in a glass: for he beholdeth himself, and goeth his way, and straightway forgetteth what manner of man he was. But whoso looketh into the perfect law of liberty, and continueth therein, **he being not a forgetful hearer, but a doer of the work, this man shall be blessed in his deed**"* (James 1:23-25). We begin to lose our identity in Christ when we hear God's Word and disobey it. Let's not forget who we are, we are children of the Most High God. If this is true, then it is time we begin to act like it!

As we observed earlier, the wise virgins were doers of God's Word, the foolish virgins were hearers only. The foolish virgins were not prepared and began to knock on the door and to call out, *"Lord, Lord, open to us"* (Matt. 25:11). Clearly these women, although not wise, were not bad people. They wanted to be with the Lord. They had their lamps, but they had just become sloppy and neglected to maintain enough oil to make them work and give their light. And now they wanted entrance to the marriage; they desperately wanted to be part of the celebration. But my friend, hear the Lord's sad reply to them that day, *"Verily I say unto you, I know you not"* (Matt. 25:12). And the warning to all of us who might be tempted to fall into the same trap is, *"Watch therefore, for ye know neither the day nor the hour wherein the Son of man cometh"* (Matt. 25:13). Luke documented it as follows: *"Watch ye therefore, and pray always, that ye may be accounted worthy to escape all these things that shall come to pass, and to stand before the Son of man"* (Luke 21:36). And Mark records it this way, *"Watch ye therefore: for ye know not when the master of the house cometh, at even, or at midnight, or at the cockcrowing, or in the morning: lest coming suddenly he find you sleeping. And what I say unto you I say unto all, Watch"* (Mark 13:35-37). Watch! Watch! Watch! Warning always comes before destruction. Will you heed God's call and choose to set your house in order today?

YOUR NECESSARY FOOD, GOD'S WORD

Thank God for food! There are countless human beings around the world who are literally starving to death. They are malnourished, underweight, emaciated, and find themselves physically wasting away. It's time to make a difference in the lives of others. It's time to change the world. Jesus wants us to feed the hungry, give drink to the thirsty, provide shelter to the homeless, and clothe those who are naked (Matt. 25:31-46). Our attitude should match the attitude exhibited by the Good Samaritan as described in the Bible. It was one of sacrifice and service to all.

> *And Jesus answering said, A certain man went down from Jerusalem to Jericho, and fell among thieves, which stripped him of his raiment, and wounded him, and departed, leaving him half dead. And by chance there came down a certain priest that way: and when he saw him, he passed by on the other side. And likewise a Levite, when he was at the place, came and looked on him, and passed by on the other side. But a certain Samaritan, as he journeyed, came where he was: and when he saw him, he had compassion on him,* **and went to him, and bound up his wounds, pouring in oil and wine, and set him on his own beast, and brought him to an inn, and took care of him.** *And on the morrow when he departed, he took out two pence, and gave them to the host, and said unto him, Take care of him; and whatsoever thou spendest more, when I come again, I will repay thee. Which now of these three, thinkest thou, was neighbour unto him that fell among the thieves? And he said, he that shewed mercy on him.* **Then said Jesus unto him, Go, and do thou likewise** (Luke 10:30-37).

The Good Samaritan showed love and mercy to a perfect stranger who had been the victim of a crime. He cared for the stranger and took him to an inn. No one asked him to do it; he did it out of the goodness of his heart. These are the kinds of acts of love and kindness that we all must proactively pursue. Loving and caring for others is a part of the Christian mandate. This love should be demonstrated without bias or prejudice. Love should be liberally bestowed upon those who come from all walks of life, regardless of upbringing, social status, economic standing, or educational background. Love should always be willing to sacrifice, serve, and give.

We have just discussed the importance of having access to wholesome food for the survival and wellbeing of the human body, as well as the attitude we must all have when showing our love for others by caring for their needs. Hopefully, we will all show a greater sense of gratitude when we are privileged enough to have access to good, nutritious, and healthful food. Not everyone does, and without it we can all quickly become frail and malnourished. Interestingly, as the human body becomes weak, anemic, and eventually dies if it does not receive proper nourishment, so also will the human spirit become weak and experience eternal death without proper spiritual nourishment. If we are to keep our spirits healthy and prosperous, we will have to actively hunger for spiritual food and consume it continuously. We will have to relentlessly pursue God's Word, God's Kingdom, and God's righteousness. God promises to satisfy our hunger and thirst for His righteousness and holiness. Jesus said, *"Blessed are they which do hunger and thirst after righteousness: for they shall be filled"* (Matt. 5:6). What is your spirit hungering and thirsting for? Is it righteousness? Is it God's Word? Is it God's will? If so, you will be filled. You will find God's will in God's Word, without which true spiritual growth is not possible. As Peter said, *"desire the sincere milk of the word, that ye may grow thereby"* (1 Peter 2:2).

Jesus understood the overriding importance of spiritual food, which is God's Word. He demonstrated how critical to spiritual survival knowing God's Word was when He faced the enemy. After being baptized by John the Baptist, Jesus was led into the wilderness and fasted for 40 days just before being tempted by the devil. The book of Matthew chronicles it this way:

*Then was Jesus led up of the Spirit into the wilderness to be tempted of the devil. And when he had **fasted forty days and forty nights, he was afterward an hungred**. And when the tempter came to him, he said, If thou be the Son of God, command that these stones be made bread. But he answered and said, **It is written, Man shall not live by bread alone, but by every word that proceedeth out of the mouth of God*** (Matthew 4:1-4).

Notice in the passage above that Jesus quoted Deuteronomy 8:3 when he said, *"Man shall not live by bread alone, **but by every word that proceedeth out of the mouth of God"*** (Matt. 4:4). Job's sentiment was similar when he wrote, *"I have esteemed the words of his mouth **more than my necessary food"*** (Job 23:12). This is the revelation that we should all embrace enthusiastically: The Word of God is vital to our spiritual survival!

The Bible teaches that Jesus and the Word of God are one in the same. In the book of John we read, *"In the beginning was the Word, and the Word was with God, and the Word was God. The same was in the beginning with God"* (John 1:1-2). Later in the same chapter, speaking of Jesus, John wrote, *"And the Word was made flesh, and dwelt among us, (and we beheld his glory, the glory as of the only begotten of the Father,) full of grace and truth"* (John 1:14). Jesus was both God incarnate and the Word of God incarnate. Thus, as we love God's Word and His commandments, we must also love Jesus. In fact, Jesus said, *"If ye love me, keep my commandments"* (John 14:15). It's clear we demonstrate our love for God when we love His Word and keep His commandments.

Speaking of spiritual food, Jesus said, *"I am the bread of life"* (John 6:35). He also said, *"I am the way, the truth, and the life: no man cometh unto the Father, but by me" (John 14:6). Eternal life can only be found in Jesus, the Son of God and the bread of life.

Verily, verily, I say unto you, he that believeth on me hath **everlasting life. I am that bread of life.** *Your fathers did eat manna in the wilderness,* **and are dead.** *This is the bread which cometh down from heaven, that a man may eat thereof, and not die. I am the living bread which came down from heaven:* **if any man eat of this bread, he shall live for ever:** *and the bread that I will give is my flesh, which I will give for the life of the world. The Jews therefore strove among themselves, saying, How can this man give us his flesh to eat? Then Jesus said unto them, Verily, verily, I say unto you, Except ye eat the flesh of the Son of man, and drink his blood, ye have no life in you.* **Whoso eateth my flesh, and drinketh my blood, hath eternal life; and I will raise him up at the last day.** *For my flesh is meat indeed, and my blood is drink indeed. He that eateth my flesh, and drinketh my blood, dwelleth in me, and I in him. As the living Father hath sent me, and I live by the Father: so he that eateth me, even he shall live by me. This is that bread which came down from heaven: not as your fathers did eat manna, and are dead:* **he that eateth of this bread shall live for ever.** *These things said he in the synagogue, as he taught in Capernaum. Many therefore of his disciples, when they had heard this, said, This is an hard saying; who can hear it? When Jesus knew in himself that his disciples murmured at it, he said unto them, Doth this offend you? What and if ye shall see the Son of man ascend up where he was before?* **It is the spirit that quickeneth; the flesh profiteth nothing: the words that I speak unto you, they are spirit, and they are life** (John 6:47-63).

Eat the bread of life! Eat the Word of life! Eat the Word of God! Let His Word dwell in you richly! (see Col. 3:16). Hide God's Word in your heart that you might not sin against Him! (see Ps. 119:11). Power-pack your spirit with the Word of God! *"Study to shew thyself approved unto God, a workman that needeth not to be ashamed, rightly dividing the word of truth"* (2 Tim. 2:15). When you study the Word of God and hide it in your heart, you will realize that when you need it most it will never let you down and you will be able to overcome any obstacle the enemy places in your way.

The Word also brings great transformation, as Paul plainly states, *"be not conformed to this world: but be ye transformed by the renewing of your mind"* (Rom. 12:2). The renewal and change that Paul speaks of only comes by the washing of the water of the Word of God which produces sanctification and cleansing in the body of Christ that all true believers are members of (see Eph. 5:26). Jesus, when praying to His Father, confirmed the sanctifying power of God's Word when He said, *"Sanctify them through thy truth: thy word is truth"* (John 17:17).

It's time to stop walking in darkness, and it's time to start walking in the light. Walk in God's Word and you will no longer walk in darkness, you will walk in the light. King David affirmed, *"Thy word is a lamp unto my feet, and a light unto my path"* (Ps. 119:105).

GOD'S FAST

Although there is no express command in the Bible to fast, there was a clear expectation on Jesus's part that His followers would fast. In Matthew, Jesus said, *"When ye fast,"* not *"if ye fast,"* when addressing the subject (Matt. 6:16). Interestingly, Jesus also spoke of the humility we must exhibit when fasting. He encouraged us to fast in secret, as opposed to openly boasting to others about what is being done.

> *Moreover **when ye fast**, be not, as the hypocrites, of a sad countenance: for they disfigure their faces, that they may appear unto men to fast. Verily I say unto you, They have their reward. But thou, when thou fastest, anoint thine head, and wash thy face; **that thou appear not unto men to fast, but unto thy Father which is in secret: and thy Father, which seeth in secret, shall reward thee openly*** (Matthew 6:16-18).

If you follow Jesus, then you are one of His disciples. Some ask: Are Jesus's disciples supposed to fast? Jesus addressed this question in the following passage.

> *Then came to him the disciples of John, saying, Why do we and the Pharisees fast oft* [often], *but thy disciples fast not? And Jesus said unto them, Can the children of the bridechamber mourn, as long as the bridegroom is with them? but the days will come, when the bridegroom shall be taken from them, **and then shall they fast*** (Matthew 9:14-15).

Now that Jesus is in Heaven, able-bodied believers are encouraged to fast. What does it mean to fast? It means to abstain from eating food for a period of time, primarily for *spiritual purposes*. For those who are healthy enough to fast, there may also be many important physical benefits that might be experienced while fasting. However, the physical benefits experienced should not be the prime reason for undertaking such an activity. The motives inspiring a Spirit-led fast should be, in their essence, spiritual in nature.

An important word of caution: if *not* done properly, fasting can be detrimental to your health. Bear in mind that some may want to consult a physician prior to fasting, in order to make sure that they are healthy enough to do so. It is helpful to know that partial fasting is also a viable option. A partial fast involves fasting some types or amounts of food, but not all. Additionally, should someone make a decision to fast *with very few exceptions* it should *not* include the fasting of water as well. Fasting water or other liquids containing water, such as juices and smoothies, can be extremely harmful to your health. Consequently, remember to drink plenty of water or nutritional juice beverages when you fast and stay continuously hydrated. For those who do choose to fast water in addition to food, make sure it is done sparingly and for very short periods of time.

Also, please know that fasting is not to be done to *"punish yourself"* or to *"work"* for God's favor or to try to *"manipulate God"* into doing or not doing something you desire. And fasting should not be done with improper motives either. In the book of Isaiah, people were fasting improperly. In the midst of their fast, they were pleasing themselves and exploiting their workers. In essence, they were not demonstrating the love of God to others, but instead they were behaving selfishly. Improper motives were at play.

> *Wherefore have we fasted, say they, and thou seest not? wherefore have we afflicted our soul, and thou takest no knowledge? Behold, in the day of your fast ye find pleasure, and exact all your labours. Behold, ye fast for strife and debate, and to smite with the fist of wickedness: ye shall not fast as ye do this day, to make your voice to be heard on high* (Isaiah 58:3-4).

As a consequence, God rebuked them forcefully. God spoke and told them that the kind of fast that He desired included fundamental acts of kindness such as setting the oppressed free and breaking every yoke of bondage. He also encouraged them to share their food with the hungry, to provide shelter to the homeless, and to clothe those who were naked. In doing these things during their fast, they would be demonstrating the love of God to others, while at the same time engaging in selfless, sacrificial acts of kindness that pleased the Lord.

> *Is not this the fast that I have chosen? to loose the bands of wickedness, to undo the heavy burdens, and to let the oppressed go free, and that ye break every yoke? Is it not to deal thy bread to the hungry, and that thou bring the poor that are cast out to thy house? when thou seest the naked, that thou cover him; and that thou hide not thyself from thine own flesh? Then shall thy light break forth as the morning, and thine health shall spring forth speedily: and thy righteousness shall go before thee; the glory of the Lord shall be thy reward* (Isaiah 58:6-8).

What is evident from the passage is that, once the people conducted the fast God's way, the blessings of God followed and the glory of the Lord was their reward.

One of the great benefits of fasting is that it helps set the stage for a time of consecration and total focus on God. It is a time in which we can give our undivided attention to Him. And with this added level of devotional commitment, the likelihood of increasing our spiritual sensibilities is heightened and we will be in a better position to listen to what the Holy Spirit is trying to say to us. Our attention should be turned away from the hunger we may feel for food, and instead toward satisfying the spiritual hunger we feel for the things of God. It is a time to draw nigh unto the Lord so that He, in turn, will draw nigh unto you (see James 4:8).

There are many examples, both in the Old and New Testament, of dedicated people of God making time to fast and seek God. They recognized the significance of fasting and understood that, if done properly, it would result in countless spiritual blessings. Moses was one of the most notable figures in the Bible who fasted periodically. On one occasion he abstained from eating food for 40 days just before receiving the Ten Commandments from God (see Deut. 9:9). Shortly thereafter, Moses came down from the mountain, after meeting with God, and saw the sins the Israelites were committing against the Lord by building a golden calf and by worshiping it. Upon witnessing this abomination, Moses broke the tablets containing the Ten Commandments. Subsequently, he fasted for another 40 days for the sins of Israel (see Deut. 9:18,25-29).

Other examples of Old Testament biblical figures who fasted and feature prominently include: Elijah, who fasted for 40 days (see 1 Kings 19:8); Daniel, who fasted regarding Judah's sin (see Dan. 9:3) and who later fasted and saw a vision from God (see Dan. 10:3); King David, who fasted when he mourned the death of Saul and Jonathan (see 2 Sam. 1:12), and when he lamented the death of Abner (see 2 Sam. 3:35), and also fasted for the son he had with Uriah's wife who was very sick (see 2 Sam. 12:16); and finally, Nehemiah, who also fasted and mourned over the wall of Jerusalem that was broken down, and the gates thereof that were burned with fire (see Neh. 1:4).

Instances of God-fearing men and women fasting in the New Testament are also plentiful. For example, Anna, who had been widowed for 84 years, fasted while serving God in the temple.

"And she was a widow of about fourscore and four years, which departed not from the temple, but served God with fastings and prayers night and day" (Luke 2:37). We learn as well that the disciples of John the Baptist also fasted (see Matt. 9:14-15). Moreover, as stated earlier, Jesus himself fasted for 40 days before He began His ministry, in effect setting the example for His disciples to eventually fast after His ascent into Heaven (see Matt. 4:1-4). After Jesus's ascension to Heaven, the apostle Paul fasted following his Damascus road experience (see Acts 9:9). Later in the book of Acts, we see that certain disciples who were at Antioch also fasted and the Holy Spirit told them to separate Barnabas and Saul to undertake a mission that God had called them to fulfill:

> *Now there were in the church that was at Antioch certain prophets and teachers; as Barnabas, and Simeon that was called Niger, and Lucius of Cyrene, and Manaen, which had been brought up with Herod the tetrarch, and Saul.* **As they ministered to the Lord, and fasted, the Holy Ghost said, Separate me Barnabas and Saul for the work whereunto I have called them** (Acts 13:1-2).

Later, these same disciples fasted and prayed again just before they sent Barnabas and Saul on their mission. *"And when they had fasted and prayed, and laid their hands on them, they sent them away"* (Acts 13:3).

Mourning coupled with fasting and a deep sense of repentance can move God. The Old Testament story of the city of Nineveh, which is found in the book of Jonah, is a prime example of this truism.

> *Now the word of the Lord came unto Jonah the son of Amittai, saying, Arise, go to Nineveh, that great city, and*

cry against it; for their wickedness is come up before me (Jonah 1:1-2).

Initially, Jonah did not obey God's command to go to warn the city of Nineveh. He then tried to flee to Tarshish, away from the presence of the Lord (see Jonah 1:3). Eventually he found himself in the belly of a fish for a period of three days (see Jonah 1:17). While inside the fish, Jonah cried unto the Lord, and the Lord heard his prayer. *"And the Lord spake unto the fish, and it vomited out Jonah upon the dry land"* (Jonah 2:10). Once on dry land, God again spoke to Jonah and instructed him to go preach to Nineveh and to warn them that the city would be overthrown in 40 days. Jonah obeyed the Lord this time and traveled to Nineveh to cry out against her wickedness. Fortunately, the inhabitants of Nineveh took to heart the word of the Lord delivered by Jonah and proclaimed a fast and turned from their evil ways.

*So the people of Nineveh believed God, and **proclaimed a fast,** and put on sackcloth, from the greatest of them even to the least of them. For word came unto the king of Nineveh, and he arose from his throne, and he laid his robe from him, and covered him with sackcloth, and sat in ashes. And he caused it to be proclaimed and published through Nineveh by the decree of the king and his nobles, saying, **Let neither man nor beast, herd nor flock, taste any thing: let them not feed, nor drink water:** but let man and beast be covered with sackcloth, and cry mightily unto God: yea, let them turn every one from his evil way, and from the violence that is in their hands. Who can tell if God will turn and repent, and turn away from his fierce anger, that we perish not?* (Jonah 3:5-9)

Because the Ninevites mourned, fasted, and ultimately repented of their evil doings, God spared them the judgment they were slated to receive. *"And God saw their works, that they turned from their evil way; and God repented of the evil, that he had said that he would do unto them; and he did it not"* (Jonah 3:10).

Another great benefit of fasting is that it can help to build our faith. In the New Testament there are a set of events that highlight this point. The account describes Jesus's disciples who at one point were unable to cast out a devil from a young boy who had been experiencing seizures and suffering greatly. The child's father eventually brought his son before Jesus and begged Him to have mercy and to heal him. Jesus immediately rebuked the demon tormenting the child, it came out of the boy instantly, and he was completely healed. The disciples asked Jesus why it was that they had failed to cast the demon out:

> *And Jesus said unto them,* **Because of your unbelief:** *for verily I say unto you, If ye have faith as a grain of mustard seed, ye shall say unto this mountain, Remove hence to yonder place; and it shall remove; and nothing shall be impossible unto you.* **Howbeit this kind goeth not out but by prayer and fasting** (Matthew 17:20-21).

It was clearly because of their unbelief and lack of faith that they were unable to cast the demon out of the child. The Lord further said that *"this kind goeth not out but by prayer and fasting"* (Matt. 17:21). Jesus was underscoring the powerful role that prayer and fasting play in countering bouts of doubt and unbelief in the life of the believer. Prayer, fasting, and reading God's Word, which builds our faith (see Rom. 10:17), always have been essential to living a triumphant and victorious Christian life. These activities increase our faith and we know that *"this is the victory that overcometh the world, even our faith"* (1 John 5:4).

To summarize, we have learned that fasting, for those who are able to participate in this wonderful practice, can result in tremendous blessing. It is an opportunity for us to deny ourselves, take up our cross daily, and follow Jesus (see Luke 9:23). When deciding to fast, we must seek the leading of the Holy Spirit and acknowledge the Lord in prayer prior to our undertaking. We must pursue God's direction. God's Word tells us to, *"Trust in the Lord with all thine heart; and lean not unto thine own understanding. In all thy ways acknowledge him, and he shall direct thy paths"* (Prov. 3:5-6). Let the Spirit of God lead us. *"For as many as are led by the Spirit of God, they are the sons of God"* (Rom. 8:14). We should use the time of fasting as a time to draw ever closer to God and to soak in His presence where we will receive strength for the battles to come, for we know that in His presence is the fullness of joy and *"the joy of the Lord is* [our] *strength"* (Neh. 8:10).

3

WHAT DOES A WARNING
FROM GOD MEAN?

B ECAUSE GOD LOVES US SO MUCH, WARNING ALWAYS COMES
before destruction. Down through the annals of time, God
has never left Himself without a witness, and He will always
have one to warn men and women of His wrath to come. We
might not like such warnings, but we need them. They represent
God's loving mercies toward us. We might not like to deliver
such warnings, but if we're called upon to do so, then it is our
inescapable responsibility.

None of us know when our last day on earth will be—only
God knows that. His Word has declared, *"The Lord is not slack
concerning his promise, as some men count slackness; but is longsuffering to us-ward, not willing that any should perish, but that
all should come to repentance"* (2 Peter 3:9). This is the reason
He raises up a voice to warn us to repent while there is yet time.
Thank God for His mercy demonstrated in this way.

NOAH WAS A VOICE OF WARNING

According to biblical record, Noah preached for 120 years, saying a devastating rain would come upon the earth, but the people
of his day turned a deaf ear to him. It was not that they couldn't
repent—they *wouldn't* repent. Still, Noah kept preaching the
same message of destruction day after day.

Now think about that! He preached the same message for 120 years, "It will soon begin to rain, so come and help me build this ark, for God has said that we will need it to survive."

But the people refused to listen. I can just hear some of them jeering, "Old man, you've been preaching that same thing since we were children. It's time for a new message. More than a hundred years have passed, and it's a new day, so get a new message already. In all this time, no destruction has come, so stop crying wolf! Stop trying to scare us into believing in your God!" The reason they didn't believe him was that it had never rained on the earth before this time (see Gen. 2:5-6)

But Noah knew what he was talking about, for God Himself had said to him, *"The end of all flesh is come before me; for the earth is filled with violence through them; and, behold, I will destroy them with the earth"* (Gen. 6:13). Noah could not stop preaching what he knew to be the truth, and he could not stop building the ark God had told him to build. The ark was to be the salvation for those who believed. That's why God gave Noah specific instructions about its dimensions and the materials to be used to construct it. So Noah kept on building and he kept on preaching.

One day the Lord said to him, *"Come thou and all thy house into the ark; for thee have I seen righteous before me in this generation"* (Gen. 7:1). It was time. It was too late now for more preaching, too late for any repentance, too late for mercy. All of that had been offered and rejected. As long as Noah had been preaching, there had been time, but time had now run out.

When Noah and his family finally entered the ark that day, they must have looked around at each other and shaken their heads in unbelief and dismay. There were only eight of them. Eight souls! Can you imagine that? There were just eight people out of the entire population of the earth who heeded the warning of God for that generation.

Oh yes, there were animals too. They obeyed their Creator and went in. You would have thought the birds would have had a problem with the enclosed space of the ark, but they obeyed and went in. Even the king of beasts, the lion, was there that day—he submitted and went into the ark. The elephants, as big as they were, lowered themselves and went in. The ostriches with those big, powerful, thrusting feet and legs went in. The chimpanzees obeyed God and went in.

When Noah's family and the animals were safely inside, God Himself shut the door. The shutting of the door symbolically and practically represented closure, provided protection, and ensured safety from the impending flood the world was about to experience. Now none of them could get out, but no one who was still outside could get in either. Then God released the waters: *"The same day were all the fountains of the great deep broken up, and the windows of heaven were opened. And the rain was upon the earth forty days and forty nights"* (Gen. 7:11-12). It rained so long and so hard that the floodwaters covered the earth, reaching to some of the highest mountains. The result was that every living thing that remained upon the earth died. *"All in whose nostrils was the breath of life, of all that was in the dry land, died"* (Gen. 7:22).

We often hear that God is love, God is merciful, God is compassionate, God is kind, and it's all very true. But He has called me in this hour to declare that He is also a God of justice and judgment, and there is a line that we simply must not cross with

Him. There comes a time when God has had enough, and He says, "That's it! No more!" Early on, He had said to Noah, *"My spirit shall not always strive with man"* (Gen. 6:3), and that warning is just as true today as it was in Noah's time. Why, then, do so many of us ignore this warning and press Him until we have finally crossed the line and must be dealt with accordingly?

Noah preached for 120 years that it would rain, and it hadn't happened until that moment; but now it rained and rained and rained some more. It rained for 40 days and 40 nights. Why? Because God always does exactly what He says He will do. He means what He says and He says what He means. It's only a matter of time until every single word of warning He utters through His prophets is fulfilled. Friends, we need to heed God's warnings before it is too late.

JONAH WARNED NINEVEH

As mentioned in the previous chapter, Jonah warned Nineveh. It behooves us to revisit this story because of the powerful message it conveys regarding the importance of heeding God's warnings. In every generation, God has a witness, and Jonah was called to be a witness in his day and time. God told him to go to the city of Nineveh, and when he was reluctant to obey God chased after him and produced a great fish to swallow him up so that it could come to pass. Jonah was in the belly of that great fish with all the dead sea life swishing round about him and seaweed wrapped around his head when he started crying out to God, "Oh Lord, forgive me! I'll go to Nineveh." So God caused the great fish to vomit him out.

When Jonah finally got to Nineveh, God said to the people through him, *"Yet forty days, and Nineveh shall be overthrown"*

(Jonah 3:4). A wonderful thing happened. These people did not ignore the words of the prophet and go about their business as usual. Instead, they heard the warning, believed it, and acted upon it. Knowing that their lives hung in the balance, they became so desperate before God that they set themselves to fast and pray—called by none other than the king of Nineveh. The Ninevites even put their animals on a fast. Have you ever heard of such a thing? That's right, their animals were fasting right along with them.

When the people of Nineveh believed the warning and repented, God turned away His great wrath, and what He had spoken over the city was averted: *"And God saw their works, that they turned from their evil way; and God repented of the evil, that he had said that he would do unto them; and he did it not"* (Jonah 3:10). That's what God wants. But in order to achieve it, there must first be a warning, and second there must be a response on our part to that warning. When both things occur, warning and repentance, before time runs out, God will always bless us as He did the Ninevites. He warns us in order to restore us.

MOSES WARNED PHARAOH

God sent Moses to deliver the children of Israel, and subsequently to Pharaoh to demand that he let His people go. If not, there would be grave consequences for the Egyptians. This was the last thing Pharaoh wanted to hear, because the Hebrew slaves represented great wealth to him. They were building his cities. He hardened his heart and denied Moses's request.

But God always has the last word, even with emperors, kings, and pharaohs. Before it was over, plague after plague struck Egypt until even the firstborn son of Pharaoh perished. Then

Pharaoh changed his tune. He *would* allow the people to go, he said, and they prepared to march. But no sooner had they begun their trek toward their Promised Land than Pharaoh came chasing after them with his armies, intent on bringing them back. What a foolish man he was! Who would dare to stand against the God of the universe? Before long, however, the mighty Pharaoh was watching helplessly as his finest troops floundered in the waters of the Red Sea. That day all of his horses and chariots disappeared under the waves, and God's people, untouched and undeterred, went marching on their way.

God has always had a voice crying in the wilderness, and now He has my voice and many others' crying out with warning. The question is: Will we take heed to the warning while there is yet time? He has said, "I am coming again! I am coming back, and I am coming soon! Set your house in order." Will you hear His voice today? Don't be foolish like Pharaoh was.

LOT AND HIS FAMILY WERE WARNED

Think about Lot and his stay in the wicked cities of Sodom and Gomorrah after he and Abraham split up. Angels were sent to deliver him and his family from that place, which was so corrupt that men were lying with men. When the angels went to Lot's house, the perverted men of Sodom wanted to lay with the angels, as well. The angels had to smite the men of Sodom with blindness so they could escape. They then mercifully grabbed Lot by the hand, because he seemed reluctant to leave, and led him and his family out of the city to safety.

The command to Lot and his family as they fled that place was that they should not look back. Warning always comes before destruction. "Don't look back," God said. Why? Because He was about to destroy the city. And it happened just as God had warned—as they were leaving the city, fire and brimstone began to rain down upon it. Lot's wife couldn't overcome her curiosity and her love of Sodom and looked back, and when she did the Word of God says, *"she became a pillar of salt"* (Gen. 19:26). Later, Jesus would emphatically warn us, *"Remember Lot's wife"* (Luke 17:32). In this case, there was a warning and the results were mixed. Lot and his children heeded the warning and were saved; his wife did not and she perished. What will your decision be in this day and hour? Will you heed God's warnings about the coming Day or will you continue to live life as you always have? The choice is yours.

BROTHER WILLY WAS WARNED

There are many modern-day examples I could use to show how God warns His people before destruction comes. Here's just one.

When I was a relatively young Christian, there was a young man in our church by the name of Willy. Willy was in and out of the church. One day the pastor pulled him aside and said, "Son, when will you make up your mind to go all the way with God?"

"Oh, Pastor," Willy protested, "just keep praying for me. I'm going..."

But Pastor had seen too much and he insisted, "Brother Willy, stop playing games with God. If you want to play with something, go get a toy. God is not to be played with."

"Oh, Pastor..." Willy tried to protest.

Then, with the sternest of expressions, Pastor warned him, "Brother Willy, don't let us have to roll you into the church in a casket."

"Oh no, Pastor," Willy assured him. "I'm going to get my life right. I am."

Pastor ended the conversation by saying, "Okay, Brother Willy, we'll be praying for you."

Just two months later, Pastor was called upon to preach Willy's funeral. The reluctant young man was just 22 when he died very suddenly and unexpectedly. Will you hear God's warning today? He has given us all these examples so we can turn from our obstinate ways and come to Him.

PART II

FROM THE PIT
TO THE PULPIT

4

A VERY TROUBLED CHILDHOOD

GOD HAS RADICALLY CHANGED MY MINISTRY TO ONE OF warning the nations of the coming Day of the Lord. Much has occurred in my early childhood to prepare me for this calling. Allow me to tell you about God's dealings with my life. In the last section of this book, I will tell you more about how we can all prepare ourselves for the coming days and how we can all get our hearts right with God.

GRANDMA MINNIE

My childhood was traumatic in many ways. From the earliest days of my life, two forces competed for my allegiance. On the one hand, there was Grandma Minnie, who was my maternal grandmother. She was a faithful Christian, and she did her best to instill faith in us every chance she got.

Of the nine children in our family, I was the one who loved to go visit Grandma Minnie and spend time with her. I even spent whole summers at her house. Grandma Minnie was very fond of me, and I was fond of her. We talked a lot, and she always took me to church with her when I was there.

The pastor of the church was her son, my uncle Eddie. It was in Uncle Eddie's church that I learned to play the bongos and worship God, which I absolutely loved. But I also learned a lot from Grandma Minnie's gentle spirit. She had a hard life, but she was always happy and continually praising God. She loved to talk about Heaven.

I remember one occasion in particular when I was about nine years of age. We were lying on her bed together, and as she spoke to me I watched her hand move in the moonlight. It was a very special and unique moment, one that I would often remember in the coming years. She said, "Junior, I want you to grow up loving Jesus. Those who love Him will go to His heavenly city. It's a wonderful place where there's no more death, no more pain, no more sorrow, and no more crying." I could picture Heaven just as Grandma Minnie described it.

"Child," she continued, "the streets of Heaven are paved with pure gold, and the gates are made of solid pearl." That description nearly took my breath away. What a wonderful place Heaven must be! Then she said, "Junior, we are going home to die no more."

"But the most important thing about Heaven," she said that night, "is that God Himself is there. When we get to Heaven, He will wipe away every tear from our eyes, and we will then be forever with the Lord."

Those words moved me deeply, and I suddenly had a great longing to go to Heaven. Looking into her face, I said, "Grandma...I want to go to Heaven."

"Now, now...you'll go, baby," she said.

Then I began to cry and said to her, "But, Grandma, I really want to go to Heaven." And I meant it too. She pulled me toward her, stroked my face, and reassured me that someday I would indeed be able to go to Heaven.

That night didn't end Grandma Minnie's influence on my life. Even when I took a wrong road later in life, she continued to love me and admonish me every chance she got; I know that she was always praying for me. I dearly loved her and I'm thankful to God for the influence she had over my young life.

Throughout the years I have learned that it is enormously important to stay on track, to continuously move forward in the right direction, and to always walk on the straight and narrow path that leads to everlasting life.

From time to time I, like most, have been tempted to veer off course and move in the wrong direction. To keep this from happening, we all need to have a strong, heartfelt conviction to cling to the truth no matter what comes our way. When we face challenges, we must run to Jesus and embrace His righteousness, holiness, consecration, and sanctification. Jesus said, *"Blessed are they which do hunger and thirst after righteousness: for they shall be filled"* (Matt. 5:6). He also said, *"If ye love me, keep my commandments"* (John 14:15). Keeping God's commandments not only keeps us safe, but it also demonstrates our love for God, our love of ourselves, and our love of others.

Because clinging to God's truth, regardless of circumstances, is critical to living a triumphant life in Christ, it is essential that we commit to accomplishing this endeavor with all of our hearts. Achieving this goal is always easier when one has cultivated a close relationship with Jesus Christ and is walking right by His side. What has helped me immensely throughout life is to be in constant communion with God. It is indispensible in order to experience victory over the obstacles, challenges, and temptations we all face.

Without a disciplined prayer life and a solid commitment to studying the Word of God, we forego growth and become weak in our spirits. Let us remember that our strength comes from God. We need Him desperately. In fact, I have come to understand now, probably more than ever, the meaning of the words Jesus spoke to His followers when He said, *"without me ye can do nothing"* (John 15:5).

THE UNTHINKABLE

All of my problems were intensified when our family came to a moment of extreme crisis. Somehow I had seen it coming.

One night I had a dream where my father was killed in a head-on collision. I was now 13, and Mom and I were sitting together at the kitchen table the next morning. I was troubled about my dream and knew that I had to find some way to tell her about it. "Mom," I began, "I need to tell you something."

"Yes, son, what is it?" she asked.

I didn't know how to voice the unthinkable, so I just blurted it out. "I feel like Daddy's gonna die."

This made her upset, and she said, "Don't say such a thing!"

"I can't help it, Mom," I replied.

"But what would we do if he died?" she insisted. "Why would you say something like that anyway?"

I wasn't sure why I had said it. I just knew that the dream had seemed so real to me that I had to tell her about it. "I had a dream last night," I ventured, "and, in the dream, he died in a car crash. It seemed so real that I'm afraid it's gonna come true."

She again resisted this suggestion. "Banish the thought, son!" she said. "We need your father around for a very long time."

The next morning my dad gave me a quick driving lesson in his convertible. When we had finished and I pulled up in front of our house and got out, I went around to his side, and he stepped out with both feet onto the street. Then he looked at me in a rather strange way and said, "Well, son, can Daddy get a kiss?"

I was totally shocked. Daddy was not a kisser in the best of times. He had only told me he loved me once, and even then it had been in anger, and now he wanted a kiss? I didn't know how to receive this. I stammered and stumbled over my words as I tried to respond. "Uh...well...I'm a big boy now, Daddy. I'll give you a handshake instead."

He stared back at me disappointedly with those big, cold, black eyes. Then, resigned, he said, "Okay, son." He shook my hand and left. As his car sped off, I had no way of knowing that it was to be one of the last times I would enjoy with him. Later I would wish that I had hugged and kissed him like he had wanted me to, but by then it was too late.

Some days before that, my dad, mom, sister Beverly, and I had gone for a ride. Dad and Mom sat in the front seat, and Beverly and I sat in the rear. He was in a very contemplative mood that night and seemed to be staring at the moon. Eventually he said, "Hey, watch the moon."

Mom wasn't sure what he was talking about, so she responded, "What're you talkin' about...watch the moon?"

Her intrusion angered him, and he said, "Shut up, woman. I'm talkin' to my kids." Then, turning to me and Beverly he said, "Junior, Beverly...watch the moon." We did what our father told us, and the moon did look rather strange that night. His words proved to be prophetic.

I noticed the moon again a week after my dream and that driving lesson. My friend Jimmy and I had been outside sitting on the steps of a building for a couple of hours, smoking and talking. A tall oak tree seemed to have some leaves missing in the center, and, as I watched, the moon moved into place so that it filled that empty space, fitting perfectly into the round hole where the leaves were missing. I pointed this out to Jimmy. "Hey, Jimmy, take a look at how the moon has perfectly aligned itself in the hole left by those missing leaves."

Jimmy was annoyed by this. "Man, here you go again," he said. "Every time you say something, things start happening."

"No! Relax, man," I said to him. "I mean it. Look at how the moon fits into that space. Isn't that unusual?"

He didn't want to hear any more. "I'm out of here, man," he said. And with that, he took off running disgustedly down the street, leaving me alone. I continued to stare at the moon for a moment longer before taking off to try to catch up with Jimmy. But even as I ran to catch up with him, I kept asking myself what that strange moon could mean.

Eventually I went home, and on the way I kept asking myself this question over and over again. It had to be something more than I understood—but just what, I wasn't sure.

After I got home and because it was a warm night, I took a pillow and blanket and slept on an upstairs balcony. Early the next morning Beverly found me there and shouted to Mom, "Here's Junior, Mom. He's on the balcony."

When I went to the door, I saw my mother seated, clearly shaken by something. "Come on in here, son," she said. "I have some bad news to tell you."

It was a very tense moment as I made my way toward my mother. Evidently the other children had already heard the news and I was the last to know. When I stood in front of her, Mom began to tell me her "bad news." It was indeed bad news, and it would forever change my life.

"Junior, they found your Daddy dead," she began, and then went on to tell me how it happened. He had been killed in a head-on collision in the wee hours of the morning, just as I had dreamed it a week before, but it was those few words that echoed over and over in my young consciousness:

"They found your Daddy dead!"

"They found your Daddy dead!"

"They found your Daddy dead!"

I was devastated by these words and what they meant for my life. They seemed like the worst words I could have possibly heard. I began furiously punching the walls around me. Mom and my siblings tried in vain to console me, to comfort me, and to get me calmed down, but I refused to respond to them. Instead, I stormed out of the house and walked in the rain, tears streaming down my face. "I'll never be able to say that word *Daddy* again," I said into the air. "My Daddy is gone."

Eventually, I looked up to Heaven and spoke out loud to God, "Will *You* be my Daddy now? I feel so alone." From that moment on, I have felt that God has always been with me. That's right, the almighty, all-powerful, and all-loving God of the universe, the very best Father anyone could ever hope to have, was, from that moment on, always with me.

5

GOD'S EARLY DEALINGS
WITH MY LIFE

FIRST END-TIME VISION

I WAS JUST 17 WHEN I HAD MY FIRST AMAZING VISION OF THE end times.

I was babysitting my sister's two children one night. It was about 8 o'clock by the time I put my niece and nephew to bed. Afterward, I went into the living room, picked up a portable radio, and began to surf the airwaves trying to find something I could enjoy. Not finding anything, I turned the radio off and put it down.

Suddenly, I heard the piercing, high-pitched scream of a woman. Frozen in place and looking all around, I had a hard time figuring out exactly where the sound was coming from. It didn't seem to be coming from any particular side of the house, but rather from the air itself.

As I cautiously moved toward the open window in the living room, I sensed that I was about to see something I didn't want to see. I slowly pulled the curtain back and peered outside. Was a woman being assaulted, or even killed, right outside of the house?

But there was no woman in sight. In fact, the street below appeared to be totally empty. It was all rather alarming, and my nerves tingled with the tension of the moment.

I pondered all of this for a moment, then I started to turn away from the window. But something made me turn back, and this time I looked upward toward the heavens. Just when I had begun to feel as if there was really nothing to be alarmed about, a very strange scene began to unfold before me in quick succession. First, a strange looking moon appeared, and then it actually seemed to drip blood. Then all of the stars began to fall simultaneously from the sky, and the sky began to roll up like a scroll.

After all of this transpired, I saw the woman. She had long, black hair, and she was looking up into the sky, watching everything that was taking place. In horror, she was screaming and digging her nails into her already-bleeding face.

And then I saw the others. At first there were just ten people— men and women—running in fear. Ten became hundreds and then thousands. Everyone was running frantically, hysterically, and falling over each other. As they attempted to get up and keep running, they had a look of utter horror on their faces.

In that moment God allowed me to feel the sheer horror and total helplessness these people were feeling and thinking—that the end of time had come and there was nothing and no one who could stop what God was doing.

Just as suddenly as the vision had appeared, it was gone. I fell to my knees, trembling. "That had to be my imagination!" I said. "What I just saw could not have really happened." And yet, even as I said it, I somehow knew that what I had just seen and felt was not my imagination. It was all too real.

But what did it all mean? Still shaking, I remembered having seen a Bible in the room. As I moved toward it, fearful that I was about to see more, I begged God, "Please don't let me see anything else!" What I had already seen was more than I could bear.

Finding the Bible, I opened it, my gaze fell upon a passage from the book of Revelation, and I began to read:

> *And I beheld when he had opened the sixth seal, and, lo, there was a great earthquake; and the sun became black as sackcloth of hair, and the moon became as blood; and the stars of heaven fell unto the earth, even as a fig tree casteth her untimely figs, when she is shaken of a mighty wind. And the heaven departed as a scroll when it is rolled together; and every mountain and island were moved out of their places. And the kings of the earth, and the great men, and the rich men, and the chief captains, and the mighty men, and every bondman, and every free man, hid themselves in the dens and in the rocks of the mountains; and said to the mountains and rocks, Fall on us, and hide us from the face of him that sitteth upon the throne, and from the wrath of the Lamb: for the great day of his wrath is come; and who shall be able to stand?* (Revelation 6:12-17)

I was deeply troubled by all of this and unsure of what I should do. I desperately needed someone who could help me understand it all. The only one I could think of who might be able to help me was my uncle Eddie, who was a pastor. I quickly dialed his number.

"Uncle Eddie, Uncle Eddie," I said excitedly when he had answered, "it's Junior. Uncle Eddie, I just saw the moon turn to blood and..."

He was perplexed by what I was rattling off and a little drowsy. He said, "Whoa! Slow down, son. What's going on now?"

I tried to describe to my uncle, as best I could, exactly what had happened to me. With little pause, I asked him the question foremost in my mind, "Uncle Eddie, do you think I'm going crazy?"

He laughed. "No, son, you're not going crazy. I believe God has just given you a vision of what will take place when the end of time comes."

Wow! That blew my mind.

Then Uncle Eddie got very personal. "Junior, you know that God has called you to preach the Gospel. So when are you going to surrender to Him?"

"I'm not sure if I'm ready for all that yet, Uncle Eddie," I answered as honestly as I could. "I still like to party too much and have a good time. And you know that these two things don't go together." I truly didn't think I could live a godly life.

He asked if he could pray for me anyway, and I consented. In his prayer, he thanked God for showing me the vision and recognized that there had to be a divine purpose for it. Then he asked God to help me become willing to surrender my life to Him and serve Him, mentioning again what he called the "great future" God had for me. And he concluded with a hearty, "Amen!"

"Now, Junior," he continued, "don't forget what I said to you. Think about it, son."

We talked for a little while longer; I thanked him for his prayers and said good-bye. After I hung up the phone, I was left to ponder again all that I had seen and heard. Somehow I felt that this vision would dramatically change my future; although I could not have imagined just how the change would come or how complete a change it would be. I knew that there was something I needed to do for God before I died.

6

GOD HAS WAYS TO
GET OUR ATTENTION

GOD CALLING

ONE NIGHT I WAS STRETCHED OUT ON MY BED WITH MY ARMS extended straight out to each side. Whether I was awake or asleep I've never been able to remember. What I do remember was that I saw a woman suddenly appear before me. She had long, black hair and was dressed in a long, white robe. When I first saw her, she was coming through the side of the wall by my bed. Then she was squatting in midair, hovering over me on the bed.

"See the position you're in," she said. "This is what they did to Jesus, your Lord and Savior. They stretched Him out and crucified Him for the sins of all people. He died so that you might live. You haven't been willing to listen to a man on this subject, but you will listen to a woman. At your weakest point, God will deal with you." And with that, she went back out through the wall. From that moment on, my life seemed to further fall apart and I became desperate for some sort of solution.

Then one day I met a woman at the train station. I don't remember her name, but she had a great impact on my future.

She was a rather short, young lady from the Philippines with long, black hair. She was bold, and she approached me and very politely but forcefully began to witness to me about Christ. "I can sense that you need Christ as your Savior," she said.

I found her tone to be somewhat annoying, but I was polite to her.

"I know exactly what you're saying," I answered. "I grew up in church, so I know what's right and wrong. I've just been caught up in the circumstances of life. I want to serve God, but now just doesn't seem like the ideal time to begin."

"You know you have a call of God on your life," she said, "and you're not doing anything about it. It's time for you to make a decision to surrender your all to Him. Give Him your heart. What are you waiting for?"

I was able to put the woman off for the moment, but what she said bothered me a lot. And when I was finally alone, I cried and remembered the vision God gave me. Something had to change in my life, for I was no longer having fun. In fact, I was an increasingly miserable person.

What was the thing that finally got hold of me and helped me to escape the merry-go-round of sin? It was a simple invitation from Johnny, my friend at work. One day he invited me to go to his church for a revival meeting, and I somehow couldn't say no to him. He had a way of disarming me with his humor.

"Say, man," he said that day, "we're having revival at our church, and I'd love for you to come. How about it?"

"Oh, thanks for inviting me, Johnny," I said, "but I couldn't go. I don't have anything suitable to wear."

He laughed pleasantly. "That wouldn't matter at all," he said. "Believe me, nobody's gonna care what you have on. In fact, God doesn't care about what you're wearing; He cares about your heart. What do you say? We're having a guest evangelist, and I think you'd enjoy him."

I had suddenly run out of excuses, so I answered, "Well... maybe I *will* come."

And I did.

The meeting was already in progress by the time I arrived, and I found a seat near the rear of the church. When it came time for the preaching, I listened with great interest. I liked what the preacher was saying and I felt God in that place. When the altar call was given, I really wanted to go forward, but I wondered if I could live the life that would be expected of me if I accepted Christ as my Savior.

Probably not, I concluded. I had become too attached to the life of pleasure, so I held back.

After the service, the pastor of the church was at the door greeting people as they left. He spoke to me. "God bless you," he said. "Thank you for coming tonight. We're so glad to have you. Always remember, this is the House of God, where everybody is somebody."

Up until that point, I had been rather uptight about the whole visit, but now a smile broke across my face and I relaxed and enjoyed the conversation. "Everybody is somebody." I liked that, and I liked this pastor. He had a glow about him. He didn't make me feel uncomfortable at all. In fact, he was very warm and easy to approach. *If only my own father had been more like this man*, I thought. *My life might have turned out very differently.*

"So, son," the pastor had not finished, "will you be coming back tomorrow night?"

I surprised myself with my answer, "Well, Pastor…yes, I think I will."

I had forgotten that it was Thursday, which meant that the next night would be Friday—my biggest party night. I had to work to earn a living, but Friday night brought an end to the work week, a break from the struggle to exist, and an escape into pleasure. I began to wonder why I said I would go back the next night and to wish that I had not made that commitment.

My Life Hangs in the Balance, Again

The day after the revival, I was working on the assembly line at Ford when my boss came by and handed me my paycheck. "Here's your paycheck," he said. "Don't spend it all in one place." The minute my boss handed me that check, my first thought was to get it cashed and get my brothers together for a good party that night. Then I remembered my promise to the preacher to go back to the meeting. Why on earth had I ever promised to go to church on a Friday night? That was a crazy thing to do. I had gone to church on many occasions as a child when my mom would take us. As I got older and became a teenager my mom would ask us to go to church often. However, I would only attend about once a year, on Easter Sunday. To go to church on Friday? Never! That was always my night—a party night.

As I went about my work that afternoon, I struggled with the decision of whether or not to break my promise to the pastor. With all of my faults, I had always been a person of my word. If I said I was going to do something, I did it. But I had money in my pocket, and it was Friday. How could I keep my promise to go to church? Eventually, my will won the argument and I decided to party that night.

It was not long after making that decision that I suddenly and unexplainably fell onto the conveyor belt. As it carried me along, car parts crashed up against me, making loud noises in the process. People came running from other parts of the building to see what was happening and to find a kill switch to stop the belt.

As I struggled helplessly to get up, I began to hear an ominous sound above the obvious noises. It was my own heart, beating wildly at first, but then slower and slower. I could hear every beat, and it seemed as if my heart was slowly but surely failing. "Oh, God," I prayed, "don't let me die here. I'll go to church tonight. I'll keep my promise to Your house. I'll go hear Your Word preached."

But the beats became slower and slower, and I could see the look of horror on the faces of those around me. Everything seemed to be moving in slow motion.

"No, God," I prayed. "Don't let my life end like this. I will go to this man of God's church. Have mercy! Please have mercy!"

At that moment, my heart actually stopped and I took my last breath. But with that last breath, I cried out once more, "Lord, I promise that I'll go to church tonight. Please have mercy! Don't let my life be ended prematurely." There was a torturous pause... and then my heartbeat slowly returned to normal.

When the belt stopped, my coworkers anxiously gathered around me. One of them asked, "Are you okay?" I didn't answer him or the others who voiced their concern. I was totally focused on the Lord. "Don't do me like this," I continued to pray. "I'll go to this man of God's church."

Before returning to their work that day, my coworkers congratulated me on being saved from the accident. I was elated. I was not only okay, but I was alive and well and determined to do God's will for the first time in my life. As soon as my shift ended, I went home and started getting ready to go to church that night.

While I was preparing for church, some of my friends—Johnny, Terry, and Raymond—pulled up in the driveway. Raymond shouted, "Hey, man, let's get this party started." And they began jumping out of their cars. I went out on the porch where they could hear me and said, "Hold it! Hold it! I'm not going out tonight!"

They said, "What's up, man? What's up with you? You done lost your mind?"

I said, "I'm going to church tonight." They were confounded by my declaration.

Johnny said, "You're what? Man...you're crazy! It's Friday night. We always party on Friday night!"

"No, really!" I told them. "I'm going to church."

Still not able to understand what I was doing, Raymond asked, "But why would you do *that*? What's wrong?"

"Nothing's wrong," I answered. "It's just that you don't know what happened to me today. I nearly died. You can't keep my heart beating; only God can do that. And you can't save me; only God can do that. So, I'm going to church because I need to be saved."

They were all stunned speechless by these words. My friends didn't have an answer for me this time, so they left. I went to church as I had promised the preacher I would, and more importantly as I had promised God.

FINALLY SURRENDERING TO CHRIST

The service was, once again, great. And this time when the invitation was given, I took the opportunity to go forward and receive prayer. But my surrender to Christ did not come without a battle. As I was on my way down the aisle, I heard a voice saying to me, "Run as fast as you can. Get out of here. What are you doing?" But I had made up my mind and I kept moving forward. My knees became weak, I was nervous and shaking, and my palms were sweating. That walk felt like it was the longest walk I ever made in my entire life. I was so tempted to turn back, but I simply had to make it.

Another serious consideration in my mind that night was the girl who was living with me at the time. What would her reaction be to my changed life? In the end, I decided that I needed to attend to my own soul, and she would have to make her own decision.

Still, there seemed to be an invisible force trying to hold me back, but I stubbornly fought through it. I didn't understand it at the time, but I was fighting against unseen forces, what Paul calls *"spiritual wickedness in high places"* (Eph. 6:12). When I finally reached the altar, I felt something else entirely. God's presence was there to meet me.

The evangelist said, "Young man, do you want to be saved?"

"Yes, sir, I do," I responded.

He began to pray for me. In that moment, a great weight was lifted from my shoulders, and I was free from the burden of my past. I was a new creation and born into the Kingdom of God! I was a new creation through Christ Jesus: *"Therefore if any man be* in Christ, he is a new creature: old things are passed away; behold, all things are become new. And all things are of God, who hath reconciled us to himself by Jesus Christ...For he hath made him to be sin for us, who knew no sin; that we might be made the righteousness of God in him" (2 Cor. 5:17-18,21).

As I went to grab the hand of the preacher, the power of God hit me and I was thrown backward to the floor. I landed hard and with a loud noise, yet it felt like I had landed on a bed of cotton. Helplessly I looked up, and the power of God began to surge into me.

Initially, I felt it in my belly, then in my chest, my throat, and finally in my mouth as I began speaking in unknown tongues (see Acts 2:1-4). My life was forever changed that day. I felt a joy and peace I had never experienced before. I was an alcoholic, and had also taken many drugs, but I'd never had a high like this. Such peace! Such joy! And I knew it was God. I didn't understand it, but I knew that God had somehow entered into my mortal flesh. that *"the peace of God, which passeth all understanding"* (Phil. 4:7) had entered my soul.

Jesus told His disciples right before He ascended back into Heaven, *"But ye shall receive power, after that the Holy Ghost is come upon you"* (Acts 1:8). Power is authority, and now I had power to live for God because the gift of the Spirit had been given to me. Until then, this had always been the stumbling block that caused me to resist salvation. I didn't think I could live the life in my own power. But now I knew I could because Christ was living within me. Jesus said, *"For without me ye can do nothing"* (John 15:5).

And that was it. I had run from God and His call upon my life for so many years. But just like that, I had surrendered my life to the Almighty and taken my first steps in salvation. I was determined that He would now be Lord over my life. Of course, actually living the Christian life would not prove to be as easy as I had imagined, but thank God I was now on the right track.

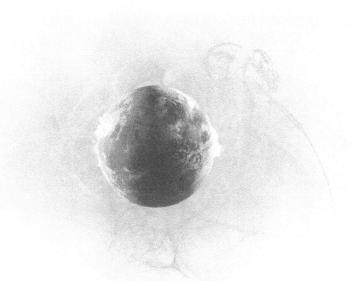

PART III

GETTING READY

7

THE DAY OF THE
LORD IS COMING

Afeter God had given me that wonderful and terrify-
ing vision about the coming Day of the Lord, He began to
show me Scriptures that dealt with this subject. As I read and studied them, I could see that what I had witnessed in the vision was
exactly what the Scriptures teach will happen. There are many of
these passages throughout the Bible, but I have included just a few
of the most important ones here for your consideration. It is not
my purpose here to go into great detail explaining what will happen on that Day, for the Scriptures are quite plain.

Probably one of the most well known accounts of the Day of
the Lord comes from the prophet Joel:

> *Blow ye the trumpet in Zion* [that's what I'm doing right
> now], *and sound an alarm in my holy mountain: let all
> the inhabitants of the land tremble: for the day of the Lord
> cometh, for it is nigh at hand; a day of darkness and of
> gloominess, a day of clouds and of thick darkness* [this is
> what I saw in the vision], *as the morning spread upon
> the mountains: a great people and a strong; there hath not*

been ever the like, neither shall be any more after it, even to the years of many generations.

A fire devoureth before them; and behind them a flame burneth: the land is as the garden of Eden before them, and behind them a desolate wilderness; yea, and nothing shall escape them. The appearance of them is as the appearance of horses; and as horsemen, so shall they run. Like the noise of chariots on the tops of mountains shall they leap, like the noise of a flame of fire that devoureth the stubble, as a strong people set in battle array.

Before their face the people shall be much pained: all faces shall gather blackness. They shall run like mighty men; they shall climb the wall like men of war; and they shall march every one on his ways, and they shall not break their ranks: neither shall one thrust another; they shall walk every one in his path: and when they fall upon the sword, they shall not be wounded. They shall run to and fro in the city; they shall run upon the wall, they shall climb up upon the houses; they shall enter in at the windows like a thief.

The earth shall quake before them; the heavens shall tremble: the sun and the moon shall be dark, and the stars shall withdraw their shining: and the Lord shall utter his voice before his army: for his camp is very great: for he is strong that executeth his word: for the day of the Lord is great and very terrible; and who can abide it? (Joel 2:1-11)

And Zephaniah describes it this way:

The great day of the Lord is near, it is near, and hasteth greatly, even the voice of the day of the Lord: the mighty man shall cry there bitterly. That day is a day of wrath, a day of trouble and distress, a day of wasteness and desolation, a day of darkness and gloominess, a day of clouds and thick darkness, a day of the trumpet and alarm against the fenced cities, and against the high towers. And I will bring distress upon men, that they shall walk like blind men, because they have sinned against the Lord: and their blood shall be poured out as dust, and their flesh as the dung. Neither their silver nor their gold shall be able to deliver them in the day of the Lord's wrath; but the whole land shall be devoured by the fire of his jealousy: for he shall make even a speedy riddance of all them that dwell in the land (Zephaniah 1:14-18).

This is the same type of situation as was described by Joel—fierce beings coming upon the earth. It will be a day like none other that mankind has ever experienced before.

Isaiah also confirmed it:

Howl ye; for the day of the Lord is at hand; it shall come as destruction from the Almighty. Therefore shall all hands be faint, and every man's heart shall melt: and they shall be afraid: pangs and sorrows shall take hold of them; they shall be in pain as a woman that travaileth: they shall be amazed one at another; their faces shall be as flames.

Behold, the day of the Lord cometh, cruel both with wrath and fierce anger, to lay the land desolate: and he shall destroy the sinners thereof out of it [there is a side of God that man has not yet experienced]. *For the stars of heaven and the constellations thereof shall not give their light: the sun shall be darkened in his going forth, and the moon shall not cause her light to shine. And I will punish the world for their evil, and the wicked for their iniquity; and I will cause the arrogancy of the proud to cease, and will lay low the haughtiness of the terrible. I will make a*

man more precious than fine gold; even a man than the
golden wedge of Ophir. Therefore I will shake the heavens,
and the earth shall remove out of her place, in the wrath of
the Lord of hosts, and in the day of his fierce anger (Isaiah
13:6-13).

John writes in the book of Revelation about the Day of the
Lord and what it will be characterized by:

And I beheld when he had opened the sixth seal, and, lo,
there was a great earthquake; and the sun became black as
sackcloth of hair, and the moon became as blood; and the
stars of heaven fell unto the earth, even as a fig tree casteth
her untimely figs, when she is shaken of a mighty wind. And
the heavens departed as a scroll when it is rolled together;
and every mountain and island were moved out of their
places. And the kings of the earth, and the great men, and
the rich men, and the chief captains, and the mighty men,
and every bondman, and every free man, hid themselves
in the dens and in the rocks of the mountains; and said to
the mountains and rocks, Fall on us, and hide us from the
face of him that sitteth on the throne, and from the wrath
of the Lamb: for the great day of his wrath is come; and
who shall be able to stand? (Revelation 6:12-17).

This again is what I saw in my vision, and the passage ends
with the great question: "*Who shall be able to stand?*" Are you able
to answer this all-important question? For if you're not able to
answer it, then it is time to get right with the Lord—today.

All of the above passages are part of the Word of God, and you
cannot pick and choose from His Word like a smorgasbord—you
either eat the whole roll or not at all. Eat what you like, but also
eat what you don't like. Eat what feels good, but also eat what

doesn't feel or taste so good. Eating it all will help you get ready for that great and terrible day.

John continues:

> *And the fifth angel sounded, and I saw a star fall from heaven unto the earth: and to him was given the key of the bottomless pit. And he opened the bottomless pit; and there arose a smoke out of the pit, as the smoke of a great furnace; and the sun and the air were darkened by reason of the smoke of the pit. And there came out of the smoke locusts upon the earth: and unto them was given power, as the scorpions of the earth have power. And it was commanded them that they should not hurt the grass of the earth, neither any green thing, neither any tree; but only those men which have not the seal of God in their foreheads. And to them it was given that they should not kill them, but that they should be tormented five months: and their torment was as the torment of a scorpion, when he striketh a man. And in those days shall men seek death, and shall not find it; and shall desire to die, and death shall flee from them.*
>
> *And the shapes of the locusts were like unto horses prepared unto battle; and on their heads were as it were crowns like gold, and their faces were as the faces of men. And they had hair as the hair of women, and their teeth were as the teeth of lions. And they had breastplates, as it were breastplates of iron; and the sound of their wings was as the sound of chariots of many horses running to battle. And they had tails like unto scorpions, and there were stingers in their tails: and their power was to hurt men five months* (Revelation 9:1-10).

Would you like to be left behind to experience all of this? I'm sure you wouldn't, for I know that I wouldn't either. So why has God revealed all of this to us? He doesn't want us to be scared, but He wants us to be prepared for what is coming. The purpose of His warning is to save us from the wrath that is to come. He warns us because He loves us so much, and it is His mercy that is reaching out to us through the warning.

His wish is that none should perish. He said, *"That whosoever believeth in him should not perish, but have eternal life"* (John 3:15). And again, He has always had a voice crying in the wilderness bringing warning. John the Baptist, for instance, in his time cried out, *"Prepare ye the way of the Lord, make his paths straight"* (Matt. 3:3).

Today God is having me cry out, "Prepare for the second coming of our Lord!" I didn't ordain myself to do this and I certainly didn't call myself to it. God Himself has called me and ordained me for this work. Therefore, I must warn men and women everywhere that time is short and that great Day is quickly approaching. I'm not alone in my warning—there is a biblical witness that has preceded me.

PRIDE RESISTS TRUTH

Pride blinds! Don't let pride keep you from seeing, receiving, and accepting the truth. Unchecked pride can keep you out of Heaven. It's what caused the devil (Lucifer) to be cast out. We should walk in humility, for we know that, *"Pride goeth before destruction, and an haughty spirit before a fall"* (Prov. 16:18). *Pride* brings a snare. It is an insidious sin that can eventually lead to our destruction. *Pride* is usually accompanied by *rebellion*, which is as the sin of witchcraft (1 Sam. 15:23). This is why we need to reject pride in our lives, humble ourselves before the mighty hand of God, and be obedient to His will, even unto death. It is a long-standing truth that, *"God resisteth the proud, but giveth grace unto the humble"* (James 4:6). Wise men recognize their fragility and, as such, are aware that they need as much grace as they can get. That is why wise men walk in humility. Only a fool chooses to be lifted up in pride. We should all be wise and walk in humility.

Because of pride, many have refused to embrace God and reject the materialistic ways of the world. On the Day of the Lord, God warns us that men will finally be forced to place material possessions in their proper perspective. Further, men will even find themselves throwing away their *silver and gold* (see Isa. 2:20). They will discard their "precious" material belongings, the same belongings they have mistakenly treasured and idolized throughout life. These are the things they have been guilty of giving undue importance. Their earthly possessions will mean nothing to them on that day. They shall appear insignificant in the face of the stark reality that the time to make things right with God is finally over. There are now no more chances, no more opportunities to repent and ask for forgiveness. This reality will drive men to try desperately to hide themselves for fear of the judgment of God. This is the very same God whom they mocked, dishonored, disrespected, and disobeyed throughout life. The day of reckoning will have arrived in which they will be held accountable for all of the evil they have done and for all of the wicked and perverse things they have said.

> *In that day a man shall cast his idols of silver, and his idols*
> *of gold, which they made each one for himself to worship,*
> *to the moles and to the bats; to go into the clefts of the*
> *rocks, and into the tops of the ragged rocks, for fear of the*

> *Lord, and for the glory of his majesty, when he ariseth to*
> *shake terribly the earth. Cease ye from man, whose breath*
> *is in his nostrils: for wherein is he to be accounted of?*
> (Isaiah 2:20-22)

As described in the book of Isaiah, the Day of the Lord will be a time when God will judge men's hearts and expose the true intentions of their hearts. On that day, *"there is nothing covered, that shall not be revealed; and hid, that shall not be known"* (Matt. 10:26). It will be a day when those who have been prideful and rebellious will finally be brought low.

> *The lofty looks of man shall be humbled, and the haugh-*
> *tiness of men shall be bowed down, and the Lord alone*
> *shall be exalted in that day. For the day of the Lord of*
> *hosts shall be upon every one that is proud and lofty, and*
> *upon every one that is lifted up; and he shall be brought*
> *low: and upon all the cedars of Lebanon, that are high*
> *and lifted up, and upon all the oaks of Bashan, and upon*
> *all the high mountains, and upon all the hills that are*
> *lifted up, and upon every high tower, and upon every*
> *fenced wall, and upon all the ships of Tarshish, and upon*
> *all pleasant pictures. And the loftiness of man shall be*
> *bowed down, and the haughtiness of men shall be made*
> *low: and the Lord alone shall be exalted in that day. And*
> *the idols he shall utterly abolish. And they shall go into*
> *the holes of the rocks, and into the caves of the earth, for*
> *fear of the Lord, and for the glory of his majesty, when he*
> *ariseth to shake terribly the earth* (Isaiah 2:11-19).

Sorrowfully, both believers and unbelievers who have been led astray by false doctrines, by erroneous ideology, by the deceitfulness of riches, by the lust of earthly pleasures, and by countless other things will ultimately recognize how foolish they have been.

Those who have dismissed Jesus's strong admonition to seek first the Kingdom of God and His righteousness (see Matt. 6:33) will forever regret the choice they made not to have done so. They will grieve over their decision to have placed other things *first* and God *last*. God help us all not to make the same mistake. Unlike them, let's make a conscious decision to always put *God first*!

BECAUSE GOD LOVES, GOD WARNS

Every act of God is motivated by love. God not only loves, but *"God is love"* (1 John 4:8). Because of God's great love for humanity, warning contained in the Scriptures has been given to all. Fortunately, some will be willing to heed the call and prepare for His imminent return; others will not.

As stated above, God's Word teaches us that the Day of the Lord will be a day when God will judge all who have rejected Him, all who have ridiculed and mocked His Holy Word, all who have derided His servants, all who have turned to their own wicked ways, and all who have refused to accept His son Jesus Christ as Lord and Savior of their lives.

Knowing the dread of this day, we should all stop doing what is right in our own eyes and start doing what is right in God's eyes. There are times when we sincerely believe that we are doing the right things and making the right choices. Nevertheless, *"There is a way which seemeth right unto a man, but the end thereof are the ways of death"* (Prov. 14:12). Let's not make the mistake of placing our ways above God's ways. Instead let us hold true to God's ways, to His Word, and to His leading. The book of Isaiah plainly states:

> Let the wicked forsake his way, and the unrighteous man
> his thoughts: and let him return unto the Lord, and he will

*have mercy upon him; and to our God, for he will abun-dantly pardon. **For my thoughts are not your thoughts, neither are your ways my ways, saith the Lord. For as the heavens are higher than the earth, so are my ways higher than your ways, and my thoughts than your thoughts*** (Isaiah 55:7-9).

God is always ready to abundantly pardon us, to forgive us, and to restore us. He desires to see us all reconciled to Him every-day in every way. He's *"not willing that any should perish, but that all should come to repentance"* (2 Peter 3:9). We may not always understand His ways or His thoughts, but this must not keep us from following His directives and mandates at all times. We must all be willing to trust Him and obey Him as He forgives us, redeems us, and leads us in the paths of righteousness for His name's sake (see Ps. 23:3).

8

THINGS THAT PREVENT US FROM BEING READY

ASIDE FROM BLATANT SIN, SOMETHING THAT MOST OF US would recognize as wrong and displeasing to the Lord, there are some specific things that can keep Christians from being ready to meet the Lord. Here are a few of the most important ones the Lord has been using me to warn the men and women of our churches about.

THE DANGERS OF UNFORGIVENESS

One of the greatest reasons many Christians are not ready for Heaven is that they have harbored unforgiveness in their hearts toward others. This is a subject that must be dealt with severely in these days. Every time I preach this message, people come to me confessing and asking for prayer. "That's me, Brother David," they say, and it happens with so many. Jesus told us to look for this very problem.

One day Jesus and His disciples were sitting together on the Mount of Olives. The disciples were excited about all of the buildings they could see related to the Jerusalem temple, but Jesus said to them, *"Verily I say unto you, There shall not be left here one stone upon another, that shall not be thrown down"* (Matt. 24:2). This got the disciples thinking, and later they approached Jesus privately and asked Him to tell them about some of the signs they should look for that would indicate His coming and the end of the world.

In answer, it should not surprise us that Jesus spoke of false christs and false prophets, of wars and rumors of wars, of famines, pestilences, and earthquakes *"in many parts of the world"* (Matt. 24:7 NLT). *"All these,"* He said, *"are the beginning of sorrows"* (Matt. 24:8). He also spoke of widespread and pervasive persecution of the saints. He then said something surprising, *"And then shall* **many be offended,** *and shall betray one another, and shall hate one another"* (Matt. 24:10).

"Then shall many be offended." This is one of the signs indicating that Jesus will be coming soon, that we are in the last of the last days of time, and that the end is upon us. People will be offended, they will betray one another, and hate one another. And I ask you today, is this not that very time of which Jesus spoke?

Because of the prevalence of the spirit of offense in our world today, the Body of Christ needs to hear this message. I always get behind a person who is telling me the truth, and I refuse to sit under any preacher who's willing to play with my soul and only tell me what I want to hear. The Bible warns us, *"For the time will come when they will not endure sound doctrine; but after their own lusts shall they heap to themselves teachers, having itching ears"* (2 Tim. 4:3). Rather than welcome the truth that makes us free, too many are saying, "Preacher, just tell us what we want to hear, and don't mention any sins because it makes us uncomfortable." Many preachers are obliging because they're more interested in numbers and offerings than in the welfare of people's souls.

When I held that 21-day meeting in Baton Rouge, Louisiana, men, women, boys, and girls came back to God, repenting and seeking forgiveness from God, then forgiving others who had offended them. One mother had been in church for 40 years and was an evangelist. She came to me after the service one evening and said, "I thank God for you, man of God, for telling us the truth. I'm going home to repent to my husband." Then she gave me one of those Holy Ghost handshakes (with some greenbacks in it).

I said, "God bless you, Mother. Go home and repent to your husband."

It should not come as a shock to any believer that the spirit of offense that pervades our world has entered the church. Good church people are not only offended, but they have come to hate each other, and they are, therefore, betraying one another. We must deal with these things.

One lady approached me wanting to be healed of arthritis in her knee. I had preached that night on releasing and forgiving others, and she said, "Pastor David, will you pray for me? I need prayer for my arthritis, but please pray for my spirit first. I have unforgiveness in my heart toward my grandma."

This lady was nearly 60 years old, so I was shocked. "What?" I said.

"When we were little girls," she explained, "Grandma was giving out candy one day. Three of us sisters approached her, and she gave my two sisters candy. But when it came my turn, she said to me, 'Get away from here, you ugly thing,' and I got nothing. I've never been able to forgive her for that." In all those years this woman had never learned the importance of releasing those who had offended her. That day, however, after she heard me preaching about releasing and forgiving others, God brought all of the hurt and pain back to her and showed her what she must do.

I said, "Let's get it straight right now, Sister. God doesn't want you to be condemned over this, but He wants you to be convicted and then do something about it. Conviction brings true repentance, and true repentance brings a change of mind and action. That's what the word *repent* means. When there is true repentance, therefore, you turn from the way you're presently going and take a new path."

The woman began to pray, "Oh God, forgive me, as I now forgive my grandma. I know she's dead and in the grave, but I forgive her today, Lord. I forgive her for not giving me any candy that day and also for calling me ugly."

When she had finished praying, I said to her, "Now let's pray for your arthritis." I prayed, and she was instantly healed.

Another lady called me for prayer one day.

"Are you the preacher who prays for people and they get healed?" she asked.

I answered, "The Lord is the Healer, ma'am, but yes, I do pray for the sick in His name."

She said, "Well my husband had cancer, and now it's come back on him, and we need God to do a miracle."

I said, "Ma'am, may I ask you a question?"

"Yes."

"Does your husband perhaps have some unforgiveness or bitterness in his heart?" I asked.

I was rather shocked by her response.

"Of course he does!" She said it with such vigor and then went on to explain that a lawyer had done him a dirty deed years before and that he had said at the time he would never be able to forgive nor forget it.

"What did you say came back to him?" I asked.

"Cancer," she said.

"Are you both born-again believers?" I asked.

"Yes, we are," she answered.

"Well, I'm not here to condemn you," I said, "but the Bible states emphatically that if you fail to forgive your brothers and sisters of their trespasses against you, then the Lord will not forgive you of your trespasses against Him. This means that your sin still remains; and when your sin still remains, you have opened the door for the devil to come in with all kinds of afflictions—even cancer. The Bible shows that when you fail to release others of their offenses, it eats at you like a worm, and, in this case, that means cancer."

I prayed for her and her husband and encouraged them to forgive the lawyer who they believed had done them wrong and release him. Life is too precious to waste on such things, and how sad it would be to miss Heaven because of unforgiveness over the wrongdoing of another person. We must forgive and move on.

That call was not unusual. Many people go to meetings where great healings take place with the desire to receive healing for all sorts of illnesses and ailments that plague their bodies, but they don't find the healing they were seeking. This occurs at times because they have not released the father who abused them when they were young, the mother who rejected them, or the brother who mistreated them. God wants you to release others, because if you don't, when that great trumpet sounds and others are changed *"in a moment, in the twinkling of an eye"* (1 Cor. 15:52) and are *"caught up...to meet the Lord in the air"* (1 Thess. 4:17), you won't be going anywhere. You'll be left standing there waiting and shouting, "Oh, wait, Lord, I wanted to go, too!"

Right now is the time to release those who have offended you. Do it now! Release them in your heart! This is the right moment—tomorrow may be too late. If you need to stop reading for a moment and pause to give yourself the opportunity to release your offenders, then do it. This is important! Forgive them now so you can receive your miracle. Release them in Jesus's name.

Jesus taught, *"Ye shall say unto this mountain, Be thou removed, and be thou cast into the sea; it shall be done"* (Matt. 21:21). He also said, *"And when ye stand praying, forgive, if ye have ought against any: that your Father also which is in heaven may forgive you your trespasses"* (Mark 11:25). That is His condition for forgiving you, so go ahead and forgive those who have done you wrong of any kind. Release them! Release them! Amen!

My dad used to beat me, but I forgave him and released him a long time ago. By doing that, I gained peace of mind. Now, when I go to bed, I sleep like a baby.

Some people still can't quite comprehend the Christian teaching on forgiveness. Are they ready to just forgive those who have done them wrong? Yes, Jesus went so far as to tell us:

> *But I say unto you, Love your enemies, bless them that curse you, do good to them that hate you, and pray for them which despitefully use you, and persecute you; that ye may be the children of your Father which is in heaven* (Matthew 5:44-45).

Jesus prayed for those who were killing Him when He had done them nothing but good, and He is calling us to follow His example. We are to forgive just as He has forgiven us.

"But why would I do that?" some insist. Well, it works two ways. When you call out the name of that person before the Lord and you begin to speak blessings over them, you are also conditioning your heart to stay in the love of God. Later, even if you happen to see that person on the street, there will be no animosity and no bitterness in your heart toward them, and you'll be able not only to greet them but also to speak with them freely. Your heart will no longer be hardened toward them. This is important—you never know what day the Lord may come.

If you have a problem with loving or forgiving, you can ask God to help you, and He will. But if you're not willing to do it, then He cannot go against your will, for He is a perfect gentleman. Are you willing to forgive others? Are you willing to forget what they did to you? Are you willing to release them from it? Are you willing to love them? If you are not willing, then nothing will happen because the Lord works only with our willingness.

Forgiveness is free, but trust is earned. Forgiving someone does not mean that you agree with what they have done. Jesus knew this when He said on the cross, *"Father, forgive them; for they know not what they do"* (Luke 23:34). It also does not mean that you have to let someone continue to sin against you or take advantage of you. You are entitled to stand up for yourself and demand respect from others. Forgiveness just means that you are releasing them in your heart for the sins they have committed, just as the Lord has released and forgiven you of your sins and commands you to *"go, and sin no more"* (John 8:11).

Now remember, the number one person you must forgive, of course, is yourself. Refuse to wear condemnation, and do not allow yourself to be condemned by the evil one. Receive readily and willingly all conviction from the Lord, but reject any and all condemnation that comes from the enemy of your soul.

Why am I telling you all of this? I'm trying to save you from the wrath that is to come. Jesus said, *"By this shall all men know that ye are my disciples, if ye have love one to another"* (John 13:35). The Scriptures also declare, *"Hatred stirreth up strifes: but love covereth all sins"* (Prov. 10:12). Yes, love can cover a multitude of sins, but first there must be a willingness on your part to forgive. Say yes to God today.

The apostle Paul reminds us, *"Let not the sun go down upon your wrath"* (Eph. 4:26), meaning never go to bed angry with your wife or your husband; never go to bed angry with your mother, sister, brother, pastor, or anyone else. Get it straight with God before it's too late.

When teaching about giving, Jesus said, *"Leave there thy gift before the altar, and go thy way; first be reconciled to thy brother, and then come and offer thy gift"* (Matt. 5:24). God refuses to receive your gift if your heart is not right with others. He's coming, and He is sending forth this warning to all the ends of the earth so that we may have time to prepare. Please do it quickly while there is time.

THE DANGERS OF LUKEWARMNESS

Another danger we face was brought to light through the great revelation given to John. Through him, the Lord said to the church of the Laodiceans:

> *I know thy works, that thou art neither cold nor hot: I would thou wert cold or hot. So then because thou art lukewarm, and neither cold nor hot, I will spue thee out of my mouth* (Revelation 3:15-16).

"Neither cold nor hot." Does that describe you? Are you just going through the motions these days? Many people are. Personally, I refuse to do so. When I received the revelation of the

Day of the Lord, I told God I wanted to be more sensitive to hearing and obeying His voice and His word. I wanted more of Him and less of me, and I asked Him to help me die to myself, to die to the way I thought. In the days to come, it must not be about what I, David, think or say; it must be all about what God thinks and says.

Many people are going to church and they have a Bible under their arm, but even as they go it is with a spirit of complacency. They were once on fire and witnessed for the Lord. They were concerned about the same things God was concerned about. They sought Him in the night, opening their Bibles frequently with genuine thirst, reading and studying with joyfulness. Consequently, God could speak to them. When it happened, tears would flow down their faces. Now they turn on the television instead and watch football or reality shows. They're enthralled with all sorts of sporting or other events, which although not necessarily bad in and of themselves have become idols because they have placed those things before God. They no longer make time for the living God. They have become complacent and unconcerned, believers in name only. They would never admit to having abandoned Him, but they are *neither cold nor hot.*

What about you? What has happened to you since you found the Lord? Do you pray like you used to pray? Do you study the Word of God like you used to? Do you fast like you used to fast? Do you still testify like you used to testify? Do you still preach like you used to preach? If not, what will happen to you now? What will become of you in the great Day of the Lord? Cry out to God today for refreshing and renewal.

The Scriptures declare: *"And because iniquity shall abound, the love of many shall wax cold"* (Matt. 24:12). It can happen to anyone, so watch that your heart doesn't grow cold. Be quick to repent. Be quick to say you're sorry from the heart. Be quick to admit that something was your fault. Be quick to take responsibility for your actions. Be quick to tell God, "It is I standing in need of prayer." And make it a point to always walk humbly before your God.

THE DANGERS OF ALLOWING YOUR FLESH TO PREVAIL

One of the most powerful things that many are allowing to prevent them from being ready to meet God is their tendency these days to pamper the flesh and let it have its own way. But God has declared that He will bless every man and every woman according to their works (see Matt. 16:27). Jesus is calling each of us to crucify the flesh and live a life pleasing to Him. Will you answer this call to come up higher?

You may say, "I'm saved!" But are you delivered? "I'm saved!" But do you have the Holy Spirit? If so, He not only gives us power and authority over all the works of the devil, but that power and authority is over our own flesh. Speak to your flesh and command it to obey God's Holy Word, to cease from its constant demands to do what it desires when it is in conflict with the will of the living God. This is why Paul told the Galatians, *"This I say then, Walk in the Spirit, and ye shall not fulfill the lust of the flesh"* (Gal. 5:16).

Even when you find yourself talking too much, you can use your own God-given authority to say to yourself, "Flesh, shut up." I know what I'm talking about because I've done it before. Many of us are guilty of running our mouths too much. When I realized that I was doing it, I took authority over my flesh and said,

"Shut up, flesh!" And do you know what happened? I shut up. You can do the same thing. All you have to do is take authority over your flesh and say to yourself, "Shut up!" You'll shut up. Try it. I guarantee that you'll be happy with the results.

An unbridled tongue is definitely one of the things that prevent us as Christians from growing spiritually as fast as we would like. Many believers and unbelievers willingly suffer from this condition that can get them into a lot of trouble. We all want to be found pleasing to our Lord at His coming; this is why we all need to bridle our tongues. After I saw the vision of the coming of the Lord, one of the things I did was to make a commitment to God to be more careful about what I say, for all of our words are powerful. Jesus said, *"For by thy words thou shalt be justified, and by thy words thou shalt be condemned"* (Matt. 12:37). Also, the Proverbs tell us that, *"Death and life are in the power of the tongue: and they that love it shall eat the fruit thereof"* (Prov. 18:21).

This is true for every Christian, even for preachers—maybe even more so for preachers. For Jesus said, *"For unto whomsoever much is given, of him shall be much required"* (Luke 12:48). There is so much power in your words, man or woman of God. So from this day forward, watch what you say. Peter taught, *"For he that will love life, and see good days, let him refrain his tongue from evil, and his lips that they speak no guile"* (1 Peter 3:10). Clearly, this is an area where the enemy is getting the better of too many of us within the Body of Christ. Rise up and take authority in Jesus's name, that you might be found pleasing in His sight when He comes.

If this secret of taking authority over the flesh works for something as simple as talking too much, try it with other areas of your life as well. You have power and authority from God, and you cannot allow your flesh to dictate your future. Put the flesh in its place and determine that you will follow God to the end, for the end is nearer than you think.

THE DANGERS OF MURMURING AGAINST YOUR PASTOR

In far too many churches today, people justify their own faults by finding fault with and criticizing their pastors. This is not hard to do, for pastors are only human, but God will not hold us guiltless when we take part in this sinful behavior against His chosen and anointed ones. Jesus states, *"Judge not, that ye be not judged. For with what judgment ye judge, ye shall also be judged: and with what measure ye mete, it shall be measured to you again"* (Matt. 7:1-2).

Many years ago, while serving as associate minister at a church I was a member of, God spoke to me about a structural change that needed to take place in the administration of the weekly services, and I decided to tell the pastor about it. After the service was over, I moved toward him but was disappointed to see that a great crowd had gathered around him so I couldn't get close to him. When the same thing happened the following week, I was discouraged.

"Lord," I prayed, "I felt like You showed me this need, and I wanted to tell my pastor." I was surprised when the Lord responded, "But you don't have to tell him in this instance; just pray to Me and I will speak to him about it."

Very often this is all we can do or should do. Don't try to control your pastor and always tell him what he should or should not be doing. That's not the will of God. If you do that, you're like a joint out of socket—you're out of place and out of order. That's not your job. God will not honor that kind of behavior. When God shows you something in the church, the first thing He wants you to do is to intercede for it and then get a word from God as to how to proceed. He may want you to humbly approach the pastor and share your observation, or He may want you to hold your peace and pray, so that either He will deal with the pastor Himself or send someone else to do it on His behalf.

The week after God had spoken to me about this matter, the pastor and I were both standing in the pulpit of the church and I was standing next to him as his official reader. Just before he began the service, he announced to the congregation that he was going to do something about the very thing that I believed God had been speaking to me about. How glad I was that God had shown him the need to do so!

Pray for your pastor. He's your God-appointed shepherd, and in these last days you will need his help as never before. A sheep without a shepherd is something to be pitied. It's helpless and vulnerable. And God has a shepherd who is perfect for your nature.

Sheep, at times, can be very vulnerable animals. They can separate themselves from the flock, and before they have wandered very far they can lose all sense of direction and no longer know where they are going or how to get back to where they were. Then if a wolf slowly moves in for the kill, the sheep are largely unaware until it is to late. They just go on munching grass, unmindful of the increasing danger that lies in their midst. When they finally become aware of the wolf's presence and sense the danger, they are paralyzed and do nothing, making it very easy for a wolf to prey on them.

Because we are in the last of the last days, it's not God's will for you to be wandering about from church to church. You need to find your designated shepherd. A true shepherd will love you, pray and intercede for your needs, give you the entire counsel of the Word of God, preach to you a fresh word from God that is relevant to you at the moment you hear it, and make the Word of God simple and understandable for you to receive with joy in your hearts. We all need God-anointed shepherds of this caliber (see Jer. 3:15; 23:4).

Some people know three Scriptures and feel an anointing and suddenly no longer believe in the need for a shepherd. As anointed as they are, sheep need a shepherd. Clearly, the ultimate Shepherd is Jesus. In fact, Jesus Himself said:

> *I am the good shepherd, and know my sheep, and am known of mine. As the Father knoweth me, even so know I the Father: and I lay down my life for the sheep* (John 10:14-15).

Nevertheless, God also sets pastors who serve as shepherds for God's flock here on earth. As long as they are following in Christ's footsteps we should also follow them. Paul the apostle proclaimed boldly, *"Be ye followers of me, even as I also am of Christ"* (1 Cor. 11:1). Some people memorize a couple of Scriptures in the Bible and they're suddenly ready to pastor themselves. Beware: the spirit of error will overtake you if you're not careful. When a true pastor is leading you, God will use him to hold off that spirit.

I can't speak for every preacher, but when I preach I'm not looking for people to like me, I'm not running a popularity contest, and I'm not angling for people's money. I'm preaching because I have a direct order from God. When people hear me preach (just as you are reading this message), I know it might be their last opportunity to respond to God—our Lord is coming very soon. Therefore I plead with them to heed the warning, for I have seen the destruction and the terror of the Lord that is coming. And this is what good men of God do.

I have memories of being in church as a baby Christian watching the pastor standing in the power of God's might and preaching the Word of God, and it tore me up. I'd wiggle in my seat. Powerful preaching hurts, but the only thing that will bring deliverance to your life is the truth of the Word of God. *"For the word of God is quick, and powerful, and sharper than any twoedged sword, piercing even to the dividing asunder of soul and spirit, and of the joints and marrow, and is a discerner of the thoughts and intents of the heart"* (Heb. 4:12). God's Word is powerful, and pastors must use it as He intended.

When any pastor does not use his God-given authority to mold and correct the sheep through the preaching of the infallible and unchanging Word of God, it weakens him, and it weakens the whole church. Some hold back because there are wealth contributors present who are giving large sums of money, and no one wants to offend them. That's a mistake, and it will get those pastors in trouble with God. Are the Scriptures not clear on this subject? *"For the love of money is the root of all evil: which while some coveted after, they have erred from the faith, and pierced themselves through with many sorrows"* (1 Tim. 6:10).

Although not always, there have been times when people have blessed me financially with the intent to control me, the church, or both, and I would not allow it. A preacher should not be for sale; ministers should be sold out to God and God alone. Because a pastor loves both God and the church, he must be true to God's

Word for the benefit of all concerned. Sometimes, people are well meaning in their desire to control the leader; however, this is outside the bounds of God's order, hierarchy, and structure for the body of Christ. When people like this have come to me in the past expressing their demands about how the church should be run, I had to say to them, "Brothers, I need to obey God. What about you?" Wherever there is a church, a flock of God's people, there can only be one shepherd leading them. Any two-headed animal is a freak of nature. The sheep should not forcibly take the staff and attempt to lead the pastor. That won't work—it's out of order and God won't bless it. The anointing of God flows with order.

Again, I must insist that there is a side of God that we have not yet known. When the children of Israel were still wandering in the wilderness and came to Mount Sinai, the Lord came down and Moses later wrote, *"There were thunders and lightnings, and a thick cloud upon the mount, and the voice of the trumpet exceeding loud; so that all the people that was in the camp trembled"* (Exod. 19:16). Until that moment, the people didn't want to heed Moses's words, but after God demonstrated His power in this new way, they said to Moses, *"Speak thou with us, and we will hear: but let not God speak with us, lest we die"* (Exod. 20:19). Moses answered them, *"Fear not: for God is come to prove you, and that his fear may be before your faces, that ye sin not"* (Exod. 20:20). It's the same today, but now God is speaking through His servants, the pastors.

We should thank God for every preacher, every apostle, pastor, evangelist, prophet, and teacher. We should thank Him, for He has set these gifts in the Church to perfect us. Ministers, therefore, have no reason to envy each other or to try to outdo one another. Instead, we should get behind each other and hold each other up. Psalm 133 shows us that where there is unity, *"there the Lord commanded the blessing"* (Ps. 133:3). We need each other. One hand washes the other.

If you are a pastor, when another is in your pulpit, get behind him. Don't just sit there like a bump on a log. You should know the forces he's facing. The devil is trying to keep him from remembering the Scriptures and where he needs to go with his message. The enemy is fighting him in every way. And I wish the congregation could be up with us to see the look on the faces of the people sitting out there in front of us. I think they'd be surprised. Love your pastors and pray for them, don't criticize them.

THE DANGERS OF PRIDE AND REBELLION

In the previous chapter I discussed how pride keeps us from receiving the truth. Pride can also affect us negatively in other ways as well. Pride and its companion, rebellion, are powerful thieves that often rob God's people and prevent us from being ready for the Lord's coming. There was another young man in our home church in Ohio. The Spirit of God would move upon him whenever he began to testify, so the pastor began giving him opportunities to minister the Word. Not long afterward, he went to the pastor's office one day and said, "Pastor, I feel like it is time for me to go out and preach. I want to do revivals on my own."

The pastor tried to caution him, saying, "That's all well and good, but don't be too hasty. You're still young. Let's pray about this for a while."

That wasn't what the young man wanted to hear. Angry, he said, "Wait a minute, Pastor. I'm a man of God just like you, and I have the anointing on my life, too."

In a calming way, the pastor said, "I didn't say you didn't, son." But the young man was now out of control and began to yell at the pastor. Trying again to calm him, the pastor said, "Okay, all right. It's all right. It's all right." However, the young man stormed angrily out of the pastor's office.

The next week, the young man was riding in a car with his two brothers, all three now Christians, when he noticed that some blood was beginning to trickle from his nose and then from his ears. He looked to his brothers for help, and they all began to pray.

Then the blood started coming from his eyes, and finally began oozing out of his mouth. "Have mercy on him, Lord," his brothers pleaded, but it was too late. The young man raised his hand and then suddenly expired. He was just 19 years old.

The biblical promise to the believer is long life: *"With long life will I satisfy him, and shew him my salvation"* (Ps. 91:16). The Scriptures also caution us, *"On the other hand, don't be too wicked either. Don't be a fool! Why die before your time?"* (Eccles. 7:17 NLT). It is possible to die before your time because of being prideful and rebellious. Remember, warning always comes before destruction. The Lord wants you to live, but the devil wants you to die. He comes *"to steal, and to kill, and to destroy,"* but Jesus said, *"I am come that they might have life, and that they might have it more abundantly"* (John 10:10).

Which will you choose? Avoid rebelliousness and live.

THE DANGERS OF RELYING ON "CHEAP GRACE"

There are some relatively new but very popular teachings in churches today about God's grace. They are dangerous because they stress only His willingness to forgive sin and fail to include our responsibility, as His children, to avoid it at all costs. "Sin is no problem," many are now insisting. "God will forgive it, so don't sweat it when you are tempted and find yourself yielding to that temptation." The Bible lends no credence to this teaching, and in no sense does it give the impression that God's grace can or should be taken as a license to sin. It does teach, however, against sin and is in favor of living holy lives before God.

There are many passages of Scripture that bear out what I'm saying. For example, Paul wrote to the Romans about this issue of sin. He said, *"But where sin abounded, grace did much more abound: that as sin hath reigned unto death, even so might grace reign through righteousness unto eternal life by Jesus Christ our Lord"* (Rom. 5:20-21). This is good news and might seem to support the idea that sin is never a problem. Paul went on, however, to write:

> *What shall we say then? Shall we continue in sin, that grace may abound? **God forbid**. How shall we, that are dead to sin, live any longer therein? Know ye not, that so many of us as were baptized into Jesus Christ were baptized into his death? Therefore we are buried with him by baptism into death: that like as Christ was raised up from the dead by the glory of the Father, even so we also should walk in newness of life. For if we have been planted together in the likeness of his death, we shall be also in the likeness of his resurrection: knowing this, that our old man is crucified with him, that the body of sin might be destroyed, that henceforth we should not serve sin. For he that is dead is freed from sin* (Rom. 6:1-7).

What did Paul say?

- Shall we continue in sin...? God forbid.

- How shall we, who are dead to sin, live any longer therein?

- So we also should walk in newness of life.

- Henceforth we should not serve sin.

- He that is dead is freed from sin.

If the message was not clear enough by that point, Paul went on to add:

Likewise reckon ye also yourselves to be dead indeed unto sin, but alive unto God through Jesus Christ our Lord. Let not sin therefore reign in your mortal body, that ye should obey it in the lusts thereof. Neither yield ye your members as instruments of unrighteousness unto sin: but yield yourselves unto God, as those that are alive from the dead, and your members as instruments of righteousness unto God. For sin shall not have dominion over you: for ye are not under the law, but under grace (Romans 6:11-14).

Paul was not finished yet. He continued in this same tone:

What then? shall we sin, because we are not under the law, but under grace? God forbid. Know ye not, that to whom ye yield yourselves servants to obey, his servants ye are to whom ye obey; whether of sin unto death, or of obedience unto righteousness? But God be thanked, that ye were the servants of sin, but ye have obeyed from the heart that form of doctrine which was delivered you. Being then made free from sin, ye became the servants of righteousness (Romans 6:15-18).

This chapter of Romans ends with these well-known words: *"For the wages of sin is death; but the gift of God is eternal life through Jesus Christ our Lord"* (Rom. 6:23). We use these words in evangelism and consider them to be directed to sinners, but from the context it is clear that they are meant for Christians. These final words are preceded by this powerful phrase: *"But now being made free from sin, and become servants to God, ye have your fruit unto holiness, and the end everlasting life"* (Rom. 6:22). This is God's will for our lives, that we be *"free from sin"* and have *"fruit unto holiness."*

What kind of fruit are you bearing these days? Are you free from sin and bearing fruit unto holiness? Or are you living a life of relying on cheap grace?

The writer of Hebrews reminds us:

> *For if we sin wilfully after that we have received the knowledge of the truth, there remaineth no more sacrifice for sins, but a certain fearful looking for of judgment and fiery indignation, which shall devour the adversaries. he that despised Moses' law died without mercy under two or three witnesses: of how much sorer punishment, suppose ye, shall he be thought worthy, who hath trodden under foot the Son of God, and hath counted the blood of the covenant, wherewith he was sanctified, an unholy thing, and hath done despite unto the Spirit of grace? For we know him that hath said, Vengeance belongeth unto me, I will recompense, saith the Lord. And again, The Lord shall judge his people. It is a fearful thing to fall into the hands of the living God* (Hebrews 10:26-31).

Willful sin on our part is clearly not something that God looks upon with pleasure or passes over lightly. In fact, it is clear that He will punish it, and very harshly at that. If you are a child of God, then start acting like it. That's what God expects of you.

In writing to the Corinthians, Paul said, *"Having therefore these promises, dearly beloved, let us cleanse ourselves from all filthiness of the flesh and spirit, perfecting holiness in the fear of God"* (2 Cor. 7:1). He also said:

> *Know ye not that the unrighteous shall not inherit the kingdom of God? Be not deceived: neither fornicators, nor idolaters, nor adulterers, nor effeminate, nor abusers of themselves with mankind, nor thieves, nor covetous, nor drunkards, nor revilers, nor extortioners, shall inherit the kingdom of God. And such were some of you: but ye are washed, but ye are sanctified, but ye are justified in the name of the Lord Jesus, and by the Spirit of our God* (1 Corinthians 6:9-11).

God's will is that we not be deceived into thinking we can continue to live in sin and have His blessings. Sadly, many are deceived in this regard today.

This teaching against the evils of sin is not new to the Church age. In the time of the Old Testament, God said, *"Depart from evil, and do good"* (Ps. 34:14; 37:27); *"fear the Lord, and depart from evil"* (Prov. 3:7); *"a wise man feareth, and departeth from evil: but the fool rageth, and is confident"* (Prov. 14:16); *"by mercy and truth iniquity is purged: and by the fear of the Lord men depart from evil"* (Prov. 16:6); and *"the highway of the upright is to depart from evil: he that keepeth his way preserveth his soul"* (Prov. 16:17).

Because we are living during the time of the New Testament, let's look at a few more New Testament passages on this subject. For instance:

> *There hath no temptation taken you but such as is common to man: but **God is faithful**, who will not suffer you to be tempted above that ye are able; but will with the*

*temptation also make **a way to escape,** that ye may be able to bear it* (1 Corinthians 10:13).

Yes, we are all tempted, but *"God is faithful."* And when we are tempted, He provides *"a way to escape."* You don't have to sin. God gives you the means to escape it and overcome it.

James, the brother of Jesus, also wrote on this all-important subject. He said:

> *Let no man say when he is tempted, I am tempted of God: for God cannot be tempted with evil, neither tempteth he any man: but every man is tempted, when he is drawn away of his own lust, and enticed. Then when lust hath conceived, it bringeth forth sin: and sin, when it is finished, bringeth forth death. Do not err, my beloved brethren* (James 1:13-16).

There is nothing good about being *drawn away* by our own *lust* and *enticed*—the end of it is only *death*. It is not to be celebrated.

Holiness is an extremely important part of our salvation, as the Scriptures teach clearly that only those who persevere to the end will be saved. Jesus said it Himself, *"He that endureth to the end shall be saved"* (Matt. 10:22). In His famous Sermon on the Mount, He also said, *"Blessed are the pure in heart: for they shall see God"* (Matt. 5:8). Who shall see God? The pure in heart. Does that describe most of the Christians you know today? Does it describe you? Will you "see God"?

God's Word admonishes us:

> *Follow peace with all men, and holiness, without which no man shall see the Lord: looking diligently lest any man fail of the grace of God; lest any root of bitterness springing up trouble you, and thereby many be defiled; lest there be*

> *any fornicator, or profane person, as Esau, who for one*
> *morsel of meat sold his birthright. For ye know how that*
> *afterward, when he would have inherited the blessing, he*
> *was rejected: for he found no place of repentance, though*
> *he sought it carefully with tears* (Hebrews 12:14-17).

After making his foolish mistake, Esau realized that he wanted *"the blessing,"* and he *"sought it carefully with tears,"* but it was too late. He had blown his opportunity. Be forewarned.

In writing to Titus, Paul said, *"Unto the pure all things are pure: but unto them that are defiled and unbelieving is nothing pure; but even their mind and conscience is defiled. They profess that they know God; but in works they deny him, being abominable, and disobedient, and unto every good work reprobate"* (Titus 1:15-16). When someone is pure in heart, his outlook on life is pure in its essence. Conversely, when someone is defiled and unbelieving they tend to pervert and distort even the purest of things. They sometimes have a hard time embracing clean, untainted, and uncorrupted feelings. The thoughts in their hearts and minds are defiled continually.

Yes, God's grace has appeared to all of humanity, Paul went on to teach Titus, but grace has come, not with the purpose of allowing us to live sloppy lives, but rather to create in us lives of holiness unto the Lord:

> *For the grace of God that bringeth salvation hath appeared*
> *to all men, teaching us that, denying ungodliness and*
> *worldly lusts, we should live soberly, righteously, and godly,*
> *in this present world; looking for that blessed hope, and*
> *the glorious appearing of the great God and our Saviour*
> *Jesus Christ; who gave himself for us, that he might redeem*
> *us from all iniquity, and purify unto himself a peculiar*

people, zealous of good works. These things speak, and exhort, and rebuke with all authority. Let no man despise thee (Titus 2:11-15).

Another passage that is often abused in this sense is an important one: *"If any man sin, we have an advocate with the Father, Jesus Christ the righteous: and he is the propitiation for our sins: and not for ours only, but also for the sins of the whole world"* (1 John 2:1-2). That's a wonderful promise, but it does not say that we must sin or that we can't help ourselves from sinning and that's why the Lord is our advocate and propitiation. In fact, these wonderful words are preceded by the phrase, *"My little children, these things write I unto you, that ye sin not"* (1 John 2:1). Not many are quoting that part of the verse these days, but it's still there. And the promise of Jesus being our *advocate and propitiation* are followed by these words:

> *And hereby we do know that we know him, if we keep his commandments. he that saith, I know him, and keepeth not his commandments, is a liar, and the truth is not in him. But whoso keepeth his word, in him verily is the love of God perfected: hereby know we that we are in him. He that saith he abideth in him ought himself also so to walk, even as he walked* (1 John 2:3-6).

These are just a few examples. Brethren, hear the voice of God, for the hour is late and the day of the Lord is fast approaching. The Scriptures are clear—grace without repentance is not biblical, and repentance without grace is not possible. It is the goodness of God that leads us to repentance (see Rom. 2:4). Let grace do its intended work in you today.

Satan's Opposition to Everything Good

In general terms, of course, it is our common enemy who does everything in his power to keep us from being ready. Right now, the devil doesn't even want you to read these words. As a long-time robber and thief, he is good at what he does. He has nothing to lose, for he has already lost and he cannot come back to God. He was the most beautiful angel in Heaven, but then he became proud and said in his heart, *"I will ascend into heaven, I will exalt my throne above the stars of God...I will be like the most High"* (Isa. 14:13-14). But God overheard what Satan had said in his heart and cast him out of Heaven.

Sadly, a third part of Heaven went with Satan that day, and now he and his fellow fallen angels, the demons, are here on the earth, wreaking havoc upon humanity. He feels no mercy for you, and he will never have any compassion for you. He is what he is and he will never change. John the Revelator declared, *"Woe to the inhabiters of the earth and of the sea! for the devil is come down unto you, having great wrath, because he knoweth that he hath but a short time"* (Rev. 12:12). He knows his time is short, and so he's out for blood.

Please receive the Word of the Lord for you today. Hear it so that your soul might live. Hear it that you might be saved from the wrath to come. Jesus is coming back again. There can be no doubt about that. The question is: Will you be ready when He comes? You cannot be trying to get ready when He appears; you must *be ready* in that moment. If not, it will be too late. Now is the time to prepare. Now is the time to get your heart right with God.

9

HOW TO GET YOUR HEART RIGHT WITH GOD

M Y FRIEND, IF GOD COULD CHANGE ME, THEN HE CAN change you, too. Why not submit your will to Him today and let Him have His way in your life? If you have been buffeted by the circumstances of life, know that God has a purpose for it. Give Him your all, serve Him today, and He will make all things right. I promise you that you won't be sorry for this decision. He is a wonderful Lord, and He will do for you beyond your wildest expectations.

You must realize that your soul is going to spend eternity somewhere. You will not miss both hell and Heaven and go to some nebulous in-between. Your soul will spend eternity in one of these two places. If you do not want to go to hell (and most don't), then that leaves you only one choice—turn to God. Turn to God and get your heart right with Him so that you can go to live with Him one day. Do it while you still have time.

COME CLEAN, CRY OUT, STICK WITH IT

Whenever you're struggling or having challenges of any kind in your life, it is imperative that you address them first by coming clean. If you never admit that you have a problem, you can never be helped. If you are not true to yourself and God, what can He do for you? He will never reject you when you come to Him in this humble and contrite way. He delights to hear you praying, "Father, I need Your help. Please help me, God! Help me to overcome this thing! Give me a willing heart. Give me a desire for more of You and less of me." Jesus declared, *"Blessed are they which do hunger and thirst after righteousness: for they shall be filled"* (Matt. 5:6). Just desiring God guarantees you a blessing.

Now, cry out to Him. There is no substitute for prayer, and because God is your help, there is no substitute for crying out to Him. If the desire is not there, cry out to Him for the desire: "Give me a desire and a hunger to run after You, God, to seek Your face, to seek Your voice, and not follow any other."

When you have made up your mind to do the will of God, stick with it. Jesus told His disciples, *"If ye continue in my word, then are ye my disciples indeed"* (John 8:31). There is a big *if* there. If you continue in gentleness, if you continue in meekness, if you continue in love, if you continue in kindness, if you continue in longsuffering, then you are God's child. If not, there is no guarantee. Make a commitment to God and then stick with it. Time is too short to play games. Show God that you mean business with Him today.

Don't shrug off this warning lightly. I warn you today because I love you and Jesus loves you. Jesus said that His wish was that none should perish: *"For God so loved the world, that he gave his only begotten Son, that whosoever believeth in him should not perish, but have everlasting life"* (John 3:16). He has loved us *"with an everlasting love"* (Jer. 31:3), and He wants the very best for our life; but He will never go against our will. You must invite Him in or He will not come in; you must want Him to come.

While here on the earth, Jesus said to those who would hear Him, *"Come unto me, all ye that labour and are heavy laden, and I will give you rest. Take my yoke upon you, and learn of me; for I am meek and lowly in heart: and ye shall find rest unto your souls. For my yoke is easy, and my burden is light"* (Matt. 11:28-30). The choice is completely up to you. Come to Jesus, you who are not saved. Say yes to the Lord.

You who don't know the Lord, don't let this day pass you by. Come to Him just as you are. If you know you're not saved and you want to be saved, you want to answer the call of God, and you want to know that you will spend eternity with Him, then this is your day. Please pray this prayer with me now:

Lord,

Forgive me of my sins.

Cleanse me. Wash me. Make me new. Make me real.

Help me to be on fire for You, to be a witness for You,

for everything is in Your hands, even my life.

I say "yes" to Your will, and I die to my own will.

I am Yours and You are mine.

In Jesus's holy name. Amen!

The Bible says, *"If thou shalt confess with thy mouth the Lord Jesus, and shalt believe in thine heart that God hath raised him from the dead, thou shalt be saved"* (Rom. 10:9). If you prayed that prayer, then God has heard you and you are now His.

SAVE YOURSELF

When I came out of my vision, the first thing I did was to begin praying for myself. Why was that? The Bible says, *"Save yourselves"* (Acts 2:40). Only then, after I had prayed for myself, did I start praying for my wife, my children, my siblings, my mother, and for other pastors. I knew I had to get Pastor David right first. Save yourself today, for no one else can do this for you.

"But I've been in church most of my life," some might say, and many mistakenly think that's enough. It's not. You can be a member in good standing in a church and still go to hell. The Bible says:

> *And I saw the dead, small and great, stand before God; and the books were opened: and another book was opened, which is the book of life: and the dead were judged out of those things which were written in the books, according to their works. And the sea gave up the dead which were in it; and death and hell delivered up the dead which were in them: and they were judged every man according to their works. And death and hell were cast into the lake of fire. This is the second death. And whosoever was not found written in the book of life was cast into the lake of fire* (Revelation 20:12-15).

It also says, *"And the devil that deceived them was cast into the lake of fire and brimstone, where the beast and the false prophets are, and shall be tormented day and night for ever and ever"* (Rev. 20:10). Do you want to spend eternity trapped with this deceiver? Please don't let this be your end. Repent and make all things right with God today.

CALLING ALL BACKSLIDERS

Now is the time for all backsliders to come back to God. He says that He is married to the backslider (see Jer. 3:14); so He loves you, backslider. Backsliding is like a dog returning to its own vomit: *"But it is happened unto them according to the true proverb,*

The dog is turned to his own vomit again; and the sow that was washed to her wallowing in the mire" (2 Peter 2:22).

I've seen this in nature, and it's positively disgusting. I owned an Alaskan Malamute. I let him into the house one day, and he proceeded to throw up on the floor. What a mess!

"Oh, Bear!" I exclaimed. "Oh, man!" Then he went over, smelled it, and decided he liked it and so ate it again. In that moment, this Scripture came back to me and the Lord said to me, "That's what My people have done. They have backslidden on Me and gone back to the beggarly elements of the world, and in this way, put Me to an open shame."

Why was God telling me this? He doesn't want us to be condemned; He wants us to be convicted so that we will change. The Bible states in no uncertain terms, *"If we confess our sins, he is faithful and just to forgive us of our sins, and cleanse us from all unrighteousness"* (1 John 1:9). The result—we are just as though we had never sinned. But you have to come to Him and take that step.

God is calling you to come back to Him because He loves you. It doesn't matter who you are, where you come from or what your background is. In fact, it doesn't even matter what you have done or what you have failed to do. He is calling you to come back! God is calling all people, whether you are a backslider or not, to come back to Him, for He says, *"And **whosoever** will, let him take the water of life freely"* (Rev. 22:17) and *"him that cometh to me I will in no wise cast out"* (John 6:37). Believe Him today and you will be restored.

Pray with me now, telling your heavenly Father today:

I confess to You my sins and backslidings and repent of them this day.

I acknowledge that Your Son, Your only begotten Son,
came into the world that whosoever believeth in Him,
and that includes me, should not
perish but have everlasting life.
I say "yes" to Your will and surrender my life to You.
For You I will now live, and You I will now serve.
I will be a witness for You everywhere I go.
I will be a witness in my home and on my job,
a witness that You are coming soon.
Now, Lord, help me live for You and glorify Your name.
In Jesus's name, amen!

BUT YE SHALL RECEIVE POWER

Repentance and acceptance of the Lord as your Savior is just the first step. Once you have repented and turned your life over to God, you should be willing to receive the gift of the *Baptism of the Holy Spirit.* This gift is for you! The presence of God's Spirit in your life will greatly empower you and enable you to comprehend God's Word. He truly is the Spirit that brings wisdom, knowledge, and understanding.

By way of introduction, the Bible speaks of several baptisms the believer is to partake of as a child of the living God. The *first baptism* is one in which the believer is *baptized into the body of Christ* by virtue of his repentance from sin and his commitment to follow Christ. *"For by one spirit we are all baptized into one body"* (1 Cor. 12:13).

The *second baptism* is the *baptism in water.* Once the believer has become a member of the body of Christ, God's Word directs him to be *baptized in water* signifying the death that has occurred to his *old life* (old man) of sin and the recognition of his *new birth* fostering a *new life* (*new man*) focused on pursuing holiness, purity, and the will of God. Let us remember that, *"if any man be in Christ, he is a new creature: old things are passed away; behold, all things are become new"* (2 Cor. 5:17). In addition, we see that Jesus directed His disciples to baptize new believers in water when He said, *"Go ye therefore, and teach all nations, baptizing them in the name of the Father, and of the Son, and of the Holy Ghost: teaching them to observe all things whatsoever I have commanded you: and, lo, I am with you always, even unto the end of the world. Amen"* (Matt. 28:19-20).

The apostle Paul's writings in the book of Romans give us greater insight into the meaning of *water baptism*:

> *Know ye not, that so many of us as were baptized into Jesus Christ were baptized into his death? Therefore we are buried with him by baptism into death: that like as Christ was raised up from the dead by the glory of the Father, even so we also should walk in newness of life. For if we have been planted together in the likeness of his death, we shall be also in the likeness of his resurrection: Knowing this, that our old man is crucified with him, that the body of sin might be destroyed, that henceforth we should not serve sin* (Romans 6:3-6).

The *third baptism* is known as the *Baptism of the Holy Spirit.* Once we repent of our sins and willingly accept Jesus Christ as our Lord and Savior, we can receive the *Baptism of the Holy Spirit.* When we are saved, we receive the *Holy Spirit*, who comes to dwell inside of us, but there is more; there is also the *Baptism of the Holy Spirit.*

In anticipation of this great promise, years earlier John the Baptist also spoke of the *baptism of the Holy Spirit*. John proclaimed in the wilderness:

> *I indeed baptize you with water unto repentance, but he that cometh after me is mightier than I, whose shoes I am not worthy to bear: he shall **baptize you with the Holy Ghost, and with fire*** (Matthew 3:11).

Jesus Himself spoke of the blessed Holy Spirit during His ministry. He referred to the Holy Spirit as *rivers of water* that would flow from a believer's *innermost being*.

> *He that believeth on me, as the scripture hath said, **out of his belly shall flow rivers of living water.** (But this spake he of the Spirit, which they that believe on him should receive: for the Holy Ghost was not yet given; because that Jesus was not yet glorified)* (John 7:38-39).

Let's learn about the Holy Spirit. The Bible teaches us that subsequent to our salvation our bodies become the temples of the Holy Spirit: *"What? know ye not that your body is the temple of the Holy Ghost which is in you, which ye have of God, and ye are not your own?"* (1 Cor. 6:19). God's Word tell us that those who listen to the Holy Spirit and obey His voice will be known as the sons and daughters of God.

> *For as many as are led by the Spirit of God, they are the sons of God. For ye have not received the spirit of bondage again to fear; but ye have received the Spirit of adoption, whereby we cry, Abba, Father. The Spirit itself beareth witness with our spirit, that we are the children of God* (Romans 8:14-16).

Gratefully, this promised Holy Spirit of God will forever lead us into *all truth*. We can trust Him because we know He will never speak anything that contradicts the Word of God. In fact, He will always support and confirm the Word of God because He only speaks what God directs Him to speak. Moreover, the Holy Spirit and the Word of God abide in perfect unity. Any voice, human or otherwise, that would speak contrary to what has been written in the Holy Scriptures is not of God and should not to be followed or believed.

> *Howbeit when he, the Spirit of truth, is come,* **he will guide you into all truth:** *for he shall not speak of himself;* **but whatsoever he shall hear, that shall he speak:** *and he will shew you things to come* (John 16:13).

The Holy Spirit not only leads us into all truth, but He also comforts and encourages us as we follow Christ. Additionally, the Holy Spirit abides with us forever and brings to our remembrance all the things that Jesus has said.

> *But the* **Comforter,** *which is the Holy Ghost, whom the Father will send in my name, he shall teach you all things, and* **bring all things to your remembrance, whatsoever I have said unto you** (John 14:26).

> *And I will pray the Father, and he shall give you another* **Comforter, that he may abide with you for ever;** *even the Spirit of truth; whom the world cannot receive, because it seeth him not, neither knoweth him: but ye know him;* **for he dwelleth with you, and shall be in you** (John 14:16-17).

Furthermore, believers receive power after they have been baptized with the Holy Spirit. What kind of power? Power to be witnesses of the new life they have found in Christ.

> ***But ye shall receive power, after that the Holy Ghost is
> come upon you:*** *and ye shall be witnesses unto me both in
> Jerusalem, and in all Judaea, and in Samaria, and unto
> the uttermost part of the earth* (Acts 1:8).

Christians should actively and enthusiastically seek the *baptism
of the Holy Spirit*. Receiving this baptism is so important that
Jesus specifically "*commanded*" His disciples to remain in Jerusalem and not depart until they had all received the *baptism of the
Holy Spirit*.

> *And, being assembled together with them,* ***commanded
> them*** *that they should not depart from Jerusalem, but
> wait for the pRomansise of the Father, which, saith he,
> ye have heard of me. For John truly baptized with water;
> but ye shall be* ***baptized with the Holy Ghost not many
> days hence*** (Acts 1:4-5).

After the day of Pentecost, many Christians also experienced
the *Baptism in the Holy Spirit*. One example of this is chronicled
in the book of Acts. After Jesus's resurrection, Paul the apostle
encountered believers who had not yet been *Baptized with the
Holy Spirit*. In fact, they had not even heard of the Holy Spirit.

> *And it came to pass, that, while Apollos was at Corinth,
> Paul having passed through the upper coasts came to
> Ephesus: and finding certain disciples, he said unto them,*
> ***Have ye received the Holy Ghost since ye believed?***
> *And they said unto him,* ***We have not so much as heard
> whether there be any Holy Ghost***. *And he said unto
> them, Unto what then were ye baptized? And they said,
> Unto John's baptism. Then said Paul, John verily baptized
> with the baptism of repentance, saying unto the people,
> that they should believe on him which should come after*

him, that is, on Christ Jesus. When they heard this, they were baptized in the name of the Lord Jesus. And when Paul had laid his hands upon them, **the Holy Ghost came on them; and they spake with tongues, and prophesied** (Acts 19:1-6).

Notice that these believers *spoke with tongues* once the Holy Spirit had come upon them. Similarly, we observe that Jesus's disciples also *spoke with other tongues* once they had been *Baptized with the Holy Spirit.*

And when **the day of Pentecost** *was fully come, they were all with one accord in one place. And suddenly there came a sound from heaven as of a rushing mighty wind, and it filled all the house where they were sitting. And there appeared unto them* **cloven tongues like as of fire, and it sat upon each of them. And they were all filled with the Holy Ghost, and began to speak with other tongues, as the Spirit gave them utterance** (Acts 2:1-4).

Notably, after they had all been *Baptized with the Holy Spirit,* speaking with other tongues naturally followed. What are tongues you may ask? *Tongues* are nothing more than *languages* utilized by different members of God's creation to communicate. Among these members are *humans beings,* created in the image of God, and angels, which form part of the heavenly host. Paul the apostle referred to these languages (tongues) in a letter he wrote to the Corinthians when he said, *"Though I speak with the* **tongues of men and of angels"** (1 Cor. 13:1). With this statement, he acknowledged that these languages existed among God's creatures.

When you receive the Holy Spirit, you will also receive a prayer language that will assist you in communicating with God, and will help you pray when facing challenging circumstances in life. As you pray in the Spirit, by praying in tongues, you will be edified and built up in your faith, for *"He that speaketh in an unknown tongue edifieth himself"* (1 Cor. 14:4). We should pray in tongues as often as we can. Let us not forget what one of Jesus's most committed followers, Paul the apostle, wrote: *"I would that ye all spake with tongues"* (1 Cor. 14:5). Be edified; pray in tongues every chance you get.

There are occasions when Christians will speak in tongues that are unknown and not understood by others. Conversely, there will also be times when they will speak in tongues that will indeed be known and understood by others who are listening. For example, on the day of Pentecost many heard Jesus's disciples, once filled with the Holy Spirit, speaking in tongues that they all understood. This served as a sign to them that God was real.

> *And when the day of Pentecost was fully come, they were all with one accord in one place. And suddenly there came a sound from heaven as of a rushing mighty wind, and it filled all the house where they were sitting. And there appeared unto them cloven tongues like as of fire, and it sat upon each of them. And they were all filled with the Holy Ghost, and began to speak with other tongues, as the Spirit gave them utterance. And there were dwelling at Jerusalem Jews, devout men, out of every nation under heaven. **Now when this was noised abroad, the multitude came together, and were confounded, because that every man heard them speak in his own language. And they were all amazed and marvelled, saying one to another, Behold, are not all these which speak Galilaeans? And how hear we every man in our own tongue, wherein we were born?** Parthians,*

and Medes, and Elamites, and the dwellers in Mesopo-
tamia, and in Judaea, and Cappadocia, in Pontus, and
Asia, Phrygia, and Pamphylia, in Egypt, and in the parts
of Libya about Cyrene, and strangers of Romanse, Jews
and proselytes, Cretes and Arabians, we do hear them
speak in our tongues the wonderful works of God. And
they were all amazed, and were in doubt, saying one to
another, What meaneth this? Others mocking said, These
men are full of new wine. **But Peter, standing up with**
the eleven, lifted up his voice, and said unto them,
Ye men of Judaea, and all ye that dwell at Jerusalem, be
this known unto you, and hearken to my words: for these
are not drunken, as ye suppose, seeing it is but the third
hour of the day. But this is that which was spoken by the
prophet Joel; and it shall come to pass in the last days,
saith God, I will pour out of my Spirit upon all flesh:
and your sons and your daughters shall prophesy, and your
young men shall see visions, and your old men shall dream
dreams: and on my servants and on my handmaidens I
will pour out in those days of my Spirit; and they shall
prophesy: and I will shew wonders in heaven above, and
signs in the earth beneath; blood, and fire, and vapour
of smoke: the sun shall be turned into darkness, and the
moon into blood, before the great and notable day of the
Lord come: and it shall come to pass, that whosoever shall
call on the name of the Lord shall be saved (Acts 2:1-21).

As documented above in the book of Acts, Peter took this
opportunity to proclaim the good news that Jesus was unde-
niably the promised Messiah and the Savior of the world. As a
consequence, many heard the gospel and inquired as to what it

was that they needed to do to be saved and receive the gift of the Holy Spirit.

> *Now when they heard this, they were pricked in their heart, and said unto Peter and to the rest of the apostles,* **Men and brethren, what shall we do?** *Then Peter said unto them,* **Repent, and be baptized every one of you in the name of Jesus Christ for the remission of sins, and ye shall receive the gift of the Holy Ghost. For the pRomansise is unto you, and to your children, and to all that are afar off, even as many as the Lord our God shall call.** *And with many other words did he testify and exhort, saying, Save yourselves from this untoward generation. Then they that gladly received his word were baptized: and the same day there were added unto them about three thousand souls* (Acts 2:37-41).

Some would say that the *Baptism of the Holy Spirit* was only for the disciples following Jesus at that period of time, particularly during or immediately after His resurrection and ascension. But remember Peter said that the gift of the Holy Spirit would be available to all whom the Lord our God would call. This means that the Holy Spirit is for you, if indeed you have chosen to turn away from your *old life* and have committed to a *new life* of following Jesus.

If you are a believer and have not received the *Baptism of the Holy Spirit,* all you have to do is ask God and you will receive Him. Remember, Jesus said, *"Ask, and it shall be given you; seek, and ye shall find; knock, and it shall be opened unto you"* (Matt. 7:7). I encourage you to open up your heart, have faith in God, and receive the gift of the *Baptism of the Holy Spirit!*

CALLING ALL CHRISTIANS

Now I must return to Christians. Christian, I am compelled to warn *you* this day—whatever you need to do, you must do it now, for time is winding up and quickly coming to a close. Please take heed to this warning! Your Lord is soon to come, and the Day of the Lord is fast approaching upon all humanity. I cannot be silent about these things, for God has commissioned me to warn all mankind of His coming. He showed me the visions, catapulting me into the future to show me what is to come upon the earth. With that vision, He gave me a mandate: I must warn all mankind. That includes you. Please hear this warning.

In my vision, the one young man was saying, "I thought I had time! I thought I had time!" but time had run out for all humanity. God is saying to us all today, "I'm coming for a church that has *'made herself ready'* (Rev. 19:7) and is without *'spot, or wrinkle, or any such thing'*" (Eph. 5:27).

God allowed me to see the Day of the Lord, and it is surely coming, people of God! It's coming. Are you ready? Are you ready to receive Him? Personally, I want to see His face in peace! I want to be found serving. I want to be found doing the will of my Father. If that is your desire too, then set your house in order, stay on fire for God, and lift up the name of Jesus in all that you do.

CALLING ALL PREACHERS OF THE GOSPEL

The call is also for preachers. You who are preachers of this glorious Gospel, once you have made sure your soul is ready, join us in warning all mankind of the coming judgment. Obey the Lord's admonition to you:

Preach the word; be instant in season, out of season; reprove, rebuke, exhort with all long suffering and doctrine. For the time will come when they will not endure sound doctrine; but after their own lusts shall they heap to themselves teachers, having itching ears (2 Timothy 4:2-3).

Today the cry from the pew is, "Make the message pliable and easy." But the true servant of the Lord will warn all mankind, whether they believe him or not and whether they receive him or not, because we must serve to please the God who has called us, empowered us, and placed us over His flock. How can we stoop to become mere people pleasers?

Personally, I want to one day hear the Lord say, *"Well done, good and faithful servant; thou hast been faithful over a few things, I will make thee ruler over many things: enter thou into the joy of thy lord"* (Matt. 25:23). I want to be able to say with Paul, *"I have fought a good fight, I have finished my course, I have kept the faith: henceforth there is laid up for me a crown of righteousness, which the Lord, the righteous judge, shall give me at that day: and not to me only, but unto all them also that love his appearing"* (2 Tim. 4:7-8).

Is what we do important, servant of God? Absolutely! He has said in the Revelation given to John, *"Behold, I come quickly; and my reward is with me, to give every man according as his work shall be"* (Rev. 22:12). What kind of reward will you have waiting for you on that day? Get busy doing God's work, and whatever you need to do, do it now. Don't wait for tomorrow, for tomorrow might not ever come. Don't wait until next week, for next week might not come. This is the day to obey God's call upon your life.

Time is coming to a close, so stop saying, "I still have time!" Whatever you need to do for God you must do quickly. Hear me this day. Whatever He has called you to do, let there be no more procrastination after this moment. No more! Procrastination, from this day forward, will only lead to judgment and destruction. Friend, you have been duly warned.

Far too many ministers are still pleasing people instead of pleasing God. They receive the adulation of the people, "Oh, Pastor/Prophet/Evangelist, you're just the greatest," but all the while God is saying, "I am not pleased with you, for you are not telling My people the untarnished truth." It is only the truth that will make people free.

Because of the influence of my father, I became an alcoholic early in life. When I frequented the nightclubs, I would often tell the bartender, "Give me a Hennessy, and give it to me straight. Don't dilute it. I want to feel the full effects!" Well, when people come to the house of God, you must be able to stand tall in Him and preach to them the uncompromised truth of His Gospel. When it is diluted for any reason, it loses its effect; it loses its authority and power.

Despite the fact that I have been in the ministry these many years, I still pray, "Lord, please don't let me get away from You. Please don't let me be lifted up in pride. Please, Lord, I don't want You to have to humble me. I want to humble myself." Can we, preachers of the Gospel, make any less effort at being ready for the soon coming of Christ than we expect of others? No, we must do more, for we are to set the example for others to follow. *"For unto whomsoever much is given, of him shall be much required"* (Luke 12:48).

NOW BE CAREFUL

To all of us, God is saying that we must be more careful about how we live from day to day. One day I was praying at home and God dropped a song into my heart and told me to sing it to His people. It goes like this:

Be careful what you say.
Be careful what you do.
For the Lord, He's up above, and
He's looking down on you.
Be careful where you go.
Be careful what you do.
For the Lord, He's up above, looking down on you.
He knows your thoughts.
He knows your heart.
And He knows the way that you take.
Be careful! Be careful! Be careful!
For the Lord, He's up above, and
He's looking down on you.
And You have to be careful my friend.

If you are serious about your salvation, then this song is for you. If you refuse to be denied, these words come from the Father's heart to you today. If you are determined to maintain your fire and your zeal, then let these words speak to you. It's time to live our lives more carefully, being conscious of the lateness of the hour.

It's better to be safe than sorry, for hell is hot and it is for eternity. Never worry about what other people might think or say about you, but consider only what God thinks and says. People cannot be allowed to have the last say in your life, for God will always have the last say. They can't save you, but He can. Call on Him today.

EPILOGUE

AND, SO, DEAR READER, I HAVE DELIVERED MY SOUL, AND whether you decide to serve Christ today or in the days to come, your blood will not be upon my hands. Of that I am sure.

Let it not be said that this end-time message is "all gloom and doom," as some might think. I am very optimistic about the future. Although terrible things will come upon the earth, wonderful things are in store for all those who love and honor God. For those who are washed in His blood, sealed by His Spirit, and are living a holy and sanctified life, Heaven awaits in the presence of God, for God is our ultimate reward. Furthermore, God has also promised us great blessings in this present life.

Even though a great part of humanity perished in the great flood of Noah's day, he and his family went on to be blessed and to be a blessing. Even though judgment rained down upon Sodom and Gomorrah, Lot and his children went on to be blessed and to be a blessing. You and I have nothing to fear in the future, whatever may come, as long as we maintain our relationship with the Lord and walk with Him. Whatever happens, we will be blessed and we will be a blessing. And then eternity awaits us in the glorious presence of our God. What could be more wonderful?

Always remember that we, as believers, have a hope, and that hope is in Christ Jesus our Lord. For Jesus said:

> *Let not your heart be troubled: ye believe in God, believe also in me. In my Father's house are many mansions: if it were not so, I would have told you. I go to **prepare a place for you**. And if I go and **prepare a place for you**, I will come again, and receive you unto myself; that where I am, there ye may be also* (John 14:1-3).

The *place* He is describing is called Heaven, and it is a city *"made without hands"* (Mark 14:58). Wow! When we get there, all those who have received Him as Lord and Savior will have a mansion waiting for them.

This is a place where the great promise of Revelation 21:4 will be fulfilled: *"And God shall wipe away all tears from their eyes; and there shall be no more death, neither sorrow, nor crying, neither shall there be any more pain: for the former things are passed away."* Just imagine never crying again and never having another pain. *"No more death"* because we will have glorified bodies. God has said that he will *"make all things new"* (Rev. 21:5). There will even be a "new heaven" and a "new earth" (see Rev. 21:1). In Heaven, there will be no night, no darkness, and yet no need for the sun because the Lord will be its light (see Rev. 21:23).

The city is made of *"pure gold, as it were transparent glass"* (Rev. 21:21), and *"a pure river of water of life, clear as crystal, proceed[s] out of the throne of God and of the Lamb"* (Rev. 22:1). Describing the walls, John wrote, *"And the foundations of the wall of the city were garnished with all manner of precious stones. The first foundation was jasper; the second, sapphire; the third, a chalcedony; the fourth, an emerald"* (Rev. 21:19), and there were many more. *"And the twelve gates were twelve pearls"* (Rev. 21:21), and these gates *"shall not be shut at all"* (Rev. 21:25).

Jesus said, *"I Jesus have sent mine angel to testify unto you these things in the churches. I am the root and the offspring of David, and the bright and morning star"* (Rev. 22:16). He concluded His message to the churches with this call: *"And the Spirit and the bride say, Come. And let him that heareth say, Come. And let him that is athirst come. And whosoever will, let him take the water of life freely"* (Rev. 22:17).

Jesus says, "Come!"

Amen! and Shalom!

ABOUT DAVID JONES

DAVID JONES IS A PRAISE AND WORSHIP LEADER, AUTHOR, visionary, father, and a preacher who has served in ministries for more than 25 years, 10 of those years spent pastoring a church. In 2011, God moved his ministry to North Carolina where David now resides with his wife, Suzie, and three children.

David is especially well known for his energetic praise and worship and being a man in pursuit of God's heart. As he leads His people into praise and worship, God's presence manifests and offers deliverance, healings, and salvations. When David preaches the Word of God, it is uncompromised and comes forth with a heavy anointing, authority, and power. Angels have manifested while supernatural miracles of healings and deliverances take place. Souls are saved by the power of God and the glory of God has fallen on His people.

David Jones has been featured on Daystar Television, TBN, and Sid Roth's internationally viewed program *It's Supernatural!*, as well as his international radio broadcast, *Messianic Vision*. David is a sought-after conference speaker because of the powerful move of God that accompanies his meetings.

He has also authored a book to be released in the coming months, entitled *The God Kind of Favor: How to be Irresistible to*

God. This book will reverberate with men, women, and children around the world. It clearly defines one of the indispensable virtues necessary to living a victorious Christian life. Jesus Himself demonstrated this virtue in His earthly life and ministry.

God has given David a vision—a vision with a glimpse of the near future of the end times. Now he feels the urgency to warn all mankind and to call the nations to get ready for what lies ahead.

David Jones continues to preach the uncompromised truth of God's Word and to equip the saints for the work of the ministry to bring hope, purpose, and expectancy of the supernatural power of God to the world.

AUTHOR AND MINISTRY CONTACT INFORMATION

David Jones

Little David Ministries

PO Box 480585

Charlotte, NC 28269

Phone: (704) 802-9515

Email: davidjones@littledavidministries.org

Website: www.littledavidministries.org